T0126459

Rotten
to the
(Common)
Core

Rotten to the (Common) Core

PUBLIC SCHOOLING, STANDARDIZED TESTS, AND THE SURVEILLANCE STATE

JOSEPH P. FARRELL
GARY LAWRENCE

PROCESS

Acknowledgements

No work such as this arises from a vacuum without personal experiences or the insight and assistance of others. In addition to our own experiences and research, we are grateful to Dr. Scott D. deHart for looking over this book in its earliest phases and for providing numerous insights and suggestions.

Among those who have provided us with memes and insights into the mentality of the modern administrative national security state, we are in particular grateful to Catherine Austin Fitts, former Assistant Secretary of Housing and Urban Development during the administration of George Herbert Walker Bush, who provided the key insight that Common Core's individually adaptive assessment process was the other half of ObamaCare, and deliberately designed to supplement and expand the power of the surveillance state, and is its complement to harvest that last remaining part of the local economy, in education and health care.

Finally, we would like to thank the numerous researchers, only a narrow handful who are cited in this work, who have sought to raise the alarm at the growing power of corporations and the now evident disastrous effects their policies have had on American education over the last century, of which Common Core and its assessment process are only the final end.

Joseph P. Farrell
Gary Lawrence
2016

Foreword
by Catherine Austin Fitts

I t took me two decades to face the enormity of what is happening in our educational system.

I am an investment banker and advisor by trade. I have arranged over a billion dollars in financing for major universities and educational institutions. I served on the boards of the private school and university I attended. I served on the boards of a prestigious teachers college and the government-sponsored enterprise that securitizes student loans. I started a data servicing training center and invested significantly in relational data-bases that informed the relationships between local education and real estate and property values. Despite those opportunities, I confess to being slow to see the writing on the wall.

My wake-up call started in 1998 when a group of senior employees at the CIA tried to persuade me to support George W. Bush, then governor of Texas, for President. He was going to be, they said, "the education president." I had worked in his father's campaign in 1988. George H.W. Bush had also wanted to be "the education president" but never seemed to get anywhere with it.

It did not strike me as strange that government-funded employees at the CIA were working to get Governor Bush elected. I believed that the CIA had actively worked to get Bush's father elected Vice President after he served as CIA director. Vice President Bush was responsible for running the national security, intelligence and enforcement government lines, so I had also assumed they were instrumental in also supporting his campaign for President.

So the notion that senior CIA personnel were actively working for the son just seemed to be the natural flow of events in Washington. Presumably, they had chosen education because it would help to get him elected. It was a political strategy—something to be discarded after the candidate was elected.

I remember receiving e-mail at the time from a woman who worked in a senior position at the CIA. She sent me a speech that Governor George W. Bush had given on education. Wasn't it terrific? I shot back, no, it was terrible. She replied, challenging me to explain why. I wrote back a long e-mail about what I would have said instead.

Imagine my surprise several weeks later when I opened up the paper and there was an article about Governor's Bush's latest speech on education, including an entire paragraph essentially from my e-mail, as if it were his own.

Looking back on that day, I am amazed that I did not see the dangers approaching.

When litigation with the federal government meant my company had to stop financing our data servicing training and work center in a community in Washington, I was amazed at the speed at which the Gates Foundation moved in and rebranded the project as their own. But I still did not focus on the fact that private fortunes were amassing and, in partnership with the U.S. government, were working hard in the trenches to engineer a top-down revolution in American education.

A year later, I moved to a rural area and started to hear the complaints of caring, concerned teachers struggling with efforts to drug and vaccinate children and centralize control of curriculum.

George W. Bush was indeed elected President and one of his first acts in office was to propose "No Child Left Behind" legislation on January 23, 2001, which was passed by Congress that year and signed into law in early 2002.

I was visiting Washington at the time the legislation was moving through Congress and ran into one of the political consultants who had managed Bush's campaign. The consultant kept talking about the legislation. I thought it odd—K–12 education was usually not something that fascinates hard-nosed political consultants. I failed to appreciate the enormity of the plans to privatize the educational system and the potential billions of dollars in stock market value that could be shifted to software, telecommunications and technology companies, among others, much of it at the cost of labor, local control and the quality of our children's education.

Focused on mortgage and financial fraud, it was not until the accumulated concerns of teachers whom I knew personally became pronounced that I started to pay attention. Scores of committed teachers were resigning and leaving the profession. Their reports regarding drugging of children and the impact of standardized testing were alarming.

I was—and am—deeply concerned at how invasive digital systems have become in all aspects of our lives and economy. This includes the use of entrainment and other mind control technologies delivered by media and telecommunications. It also includes surveillance and the invasion of privacy documented by numerous NSA whistleblowers and Edward Snowden. Whatever they are, digital information systems are not to be trusted when it comes to both children and adults.

That is when I started to research what was happening in education and found in Dr. Joseph Farrell and Dr. Gary Lawrence, scholars and teachers I could trust to understood both what was happening in the classroom and to help me connect it to the bigger picture.

Two of the most significant economic activities in approximately 3,100 counties that make up America are health care and education. Not coincidentally, health care practitioners and teachers represent two important aspects of what remains of U.S. middle class "backbone."

Federal mandates are requiring that health care records be digitized while the Affordable Health Care Act is essentially shifting health care financial flows into corporate hands. Digitization of records and standardization of treatment will permit more than a trillion dollars in labor costs to be squeezed out of the health care sector. This has produced quite a windfall for corporate equities as health care has lead the U.S. stock market to outperform global markets for several years

The same process is underway with the mandating of the common core curriculum and standardized testing in grades K–12. This begins the reengineering of the education process that will significantly reduce the need for and the authority of teachers.

Federally mandated reforms, if successful, will permit corporations to assume profitable ownership and control of a much greater portion of the education system: everything from software and online systems to the construction and management of charters schools. If federal legislation mandates vouchers that carry an obligation to use federally regulated curriculum, corporate involvement will likely explode.

Classrooms and online systems will soon provide direct access to children by large corporations and intelligence agencies. With the ability to integrate these flows with those coming from health care records and financial systems, the real harvesting begins.

When you look at the potential that the reengineering of health care and education systems has to create monopoly profits—both income and stock market value—you can appreciate some of the economic reasons why the U.S. leadership wanted the general population over a financial barrel. Whether deeply in debt or financially dependent on government subsidies (which are financed by debt sold to their pension funds), we are witnessing another form of leveraged buyout—one that gives highly centralized control of our children and their education to invisible forces.

If you are a parent with children in public K–12 schools in the United States, it is more important than ever *to ask whether your children* are spiritually, intellectually or physically safe *as they participate in the new educational surveillance state.* Whatever the answers, you are mandated to fund this siege on your children through your property taxes.

The reason that I am concerned for the safety of your children is because the educational surveillance state is a plan. There is a plan at the highest levels. The plan has been engineered at great expense and effort over several decades.

The plan is engineered to give direct access to your children to large corporations and intelligence agencies. It is engineered to provide that access without the intervention of teachers and school administrators that have the independence and authority to ensure nothing harmful happens.

One thing I can assure you is that the history of giving direct, unsupervised access to young children by large corporations and intelligence agencies has never turned out well.

What do you do? Do you send your children to a carefully screened private school? Do you homeschool? Do you leave the country?

I don't know. You will have to answer that question based on your unique situation.

What I can tell you is that thanks to the fearlessness and intellect of scholars and teachers such as Dr. Joseph Farrell and Dr. Gary Lawrence, you are armed with the knowledge you need to ensure a successful education for your children—now while there is still time to do so.

Preface

"Distinctions in society will always exist under every just government. Equality of talents, of education, or of wealth can not be produced by human institutions. In the full enjoyment of the gifts of Heaven and the fruits of superior industry, economy, and virtue, every man is equally entitled to protection by law; but when the laws undertake to add to these natural and just advantages artificial distinctions, to grant titles, gratuities, and exclusive privileges, to make the rich richer and the potent more powerful, the humble members of society—the farmers, mechanics, and laborers—who have neither the time nor the means of securing like favors to themselves, have a right to complain of the injustice of their Government."

—

ANDREW JACKSON, SEVENTH PRESIDENT OF THE UNITED STATES[1]

That we have profound misgivings about the new federal standards in education, the so-called "common core" standards, will be self-evident from the title of this book. Not the least of our concerns is that the implementation of these standards builds upon the power of an entrenched and privileged educational-oligarchical class, to the detriment of teachers, parents, students, children, and ultimately to the general culture. More specifically, it is our contention that the goal of Common Core, or rather, *of its assessment process*, is nothing less than a massive addition to the power of the surveillance state, to the privileged corporations destined

---

[1] President Andrew Jackson, "Veto Message to the United States Senate, July 10, 1932," James D. Richardson, ed., *Messages and Papers of the Presidents: Andrew Jackson* (No Place: Kessinger Legacy Reprints: No Date), 167–185, p. 183.

to manage it, to the further drastic curtailment of our civil liberties, and to the eventual inhibition of any individual creativity, genius, responsibility, and any general or popular intellectual culture resulting from them.

In short, the goal of the program is nothing less than Orwellian, and this, of course, constitutes an indictment of its major proponents.

During his protracted struggle against the re-chartering of the Second Bank of the United States, the seventh President of the United States, Andrew Jackson, vetoed the bill to re-charter the bank. In his veto message to Congress, he stated that the force of the bill re-chartering the bank was an implicit admission

> that the bank ought to be perpetual, and as a consequence the present stockholders and those inheriting their rights as successors be established as a privileged order, clothed both with great political power and enjoying immense pecuniary advantages from their connection with the Government.[2]

In this book we contend that the ultimate consequence of the Common Core standards' assessment process will result in the further entrenchment of the educational oligarchy, and to make it equally if not more powerful than the entrenched plutocratic interests with which Jackson contended. It will result in that education oligarchy's enjoyment of immense pecuniary benefits from its connection to the general government. We contend that the real goal is to expand the surveillance state that the American plutocracy and educational oligarchy has become.

Our argument is thus somewhat different than that leveled by many critics against the Common Core standards, for our focus is thus not upon pedagogy, or content, i.e., the standards themselves, but rather upon its *assessment process* and its implicit consequences for parents, students, and the teaching profession. We believe this process constitutes nothing less than a hidden agenda, a conspiracy if you will, against the basic standards and traditions of Western culture, and of its traditions of education. It is, as we shall argue in these pages, Orwellian in scope. It is a deliberate plan against liberty and intellectual and pedagogical freedom. In short, the Common Core assessment process and its implicit philosophy and cosmology are nothing but a conspiracy against the individual, and his or her own humanity, genius, and aspirations.

---

2   Ibid., p. 170.

Those are strong words.

And we mean every one of them in full measure.

This case depends upon the following set of interrelated theses:

1) The debate over the Common Core curriculum standards is a red herring, a magical sleight of hand, designed to deflect attention away from its follow-up assessment (testing) process, which process we believe to be the real hidden agenda of the program and its backers. It is a move away from the current fashion in "one size fits all" standardized tests in the assessment process, a process which is to be replaced by a *computerized individually adapted and individually adaptive assessment that in the end leaves the evaluation of learning outside of the hands of teachers, parents, and students.* This is the key to a dark and hidden agenda;

2) The assessment process of the Common Core standards will mean that student failures to meet the standards—especially in states with low-income, non-English-speaking students, overcrowded classrooms, or any combination of these factors—will be viewed as "teacher" failures. This "blame the teacher" meme, as we shall discover, is an old method, in use at least since Horace Mann. Its principal objective, then as now, was to drive the expansion of state power and its "edugarchy";

3) This will in turn lead to more calls for a greater role for the computerized teaching and assessments, with teachers assuming more and more the role of mere "monitors" and babysitters. The ultimate goal is to homogenize all education and pedagogy, and to remove the human and personal element, replacing them with *adaptive* written computerized instruction and assessment programs, whose adaptive algorithms are themselves the creations of anonymous experts and programmers, whose philosophical assumptions in creating the "adaptive tests" are therefore unknown, unknowable, and hence insulated from all criticism or amendment. This adaptive assessment process is the *real* rotten heart of Common Core, and therefore is the real clue to its hidden agenda, for this process combines in one mechanism both a *surveillance* system, tracking each person throughout their educational life, but also a *sorting and slotting mechanism,* used to determine the career courses and choices of individuals *en masse.* In this, the assessment process is more than a surveillance system; it is a sorting and social engineering mechanism. It will be a mechanism used to direct students into "career choices" dictated by their test results. Those accepting this state of affairs, we believe, will be given financial

incentives and favors; those bucking it, we believe, will be financially penalized for pursuing "career choices contra-indicated by their lifetime individual testing scores";

4) As a consequence of this, independent and critical thinking—the foundations of the Western cultural tradition—will be eradicated. Education will, in effect, become even more of a "soft" form of social engineering and mind or thought control than it is already. These new computerized curricula, designed in response to the implicit and, we believe, *intended* failure of the system, will be given to the already privileged testing and assessment cartels, such as the Educational Testing Service, giving even more power to the corporations and foundations involved with the never-ending process of tinkering with their tests;

5) Additionally, reliance upon computerized individually adaptive assessments will also give rise to the temptation to *replace hard-copy texts* altogether, and design *content itself* around the perceived needs of the student, such that canonical versions of texts—say of the Declaration of Independence or the Constitution—could be modified to "suit the needs of the student." Already one has a whiff of this ultimate nightmare with the various "e-book" formats being promoted, Amazon's "Kindle" being the most well-known, and egregious, example. Calling it Kindle was hardly accidental, for the objective is to "burn books," to burn canonical texts and replace them with a format (and perhaps eventually even a text) that is in constant fluctuation determined by this year's statistical results of standardized tests. The formatting of such e-books already is a blow to conventional scholarship and referencing, which requires citation of the specific *page* within a work from which a quotation or point is drawn. With formatting in flux in e-books, exactitude of citation is no longer possible; and finally,

6) We believe that another hidden and implicit goal of the assessment process is to strike against organized teachers' unions themselves, as the cost of human instruction vis-à-vis the computerized "adaptive curriculum" that will inevitably follow any such adaptive assessment process will likely be less than the expensive overhead of current education, thus tempting a "populist" revolt designed ultimately to ensnare popular support for the hidden agendas.

Our own philosophical commitment runs almost diametrically counter to all these propositions, and it may briefly be stated as follows: *there is not, and never can be, any government program, standardized test, or mechanistic philosophy or cosmology that can replace human contact, mentorship, and individual creativity and interaction in the educational process.* In short, and from this point of view, all public schools, as government programs, and all standardized tests, are failures, although, as we shall discover in the main text, there is abundant evidence to suggest that they have been *designed to be* perpetual failures. After all, it is only in perpetual failure that the "edugarchy" is permanently empowered to create ever new tests and programs, demanding more money from the government trough. Failure is essential to their power. What *success* there is in the public school system is thus not due to administrators, professional "educators" or government programs, but ultimately due to *teachers* who know their disciplines (as opposed to merely having a teaching certificate/credential) and who know how to teach and inspire students to continue their own education.

In distinction to this, the adaptive assessment process of the Common Core standards means there ultimately will be a total marginalization of role models or mentors that will inform students. We all remember our memorable teachers and professors, those who made us *think* and challenged us on the basis of their character, humanity, intellect, command of their discipline, and most importantly, whose force of individuality challenged us to rise to the full measure of our own individuality.

A Historical Approach to the Rottenness in Common Core

Our approach in this book is historical, for our aim is to expose the fact that Common Core is simply the latest trendy project to come from the bowels of the "edugarchy." To expose the rottenness within the apple of American education is not difficult. To expose the history behind how the rottenness entered in requires more work, particularly the people, philosophy, and context that has led to the rot. One would wish that the problem was accidental rather than the outcome of planned factors put into place decades ago; this would make a solution far simpler. This book cannot offer in-depth solutions without requiring that our work becomes divided into multiple volumes with the present one being little more than the outline of how we got here and why. Undoubtedly, more will be required than this volume, but the immediate need requires an immediate response, even if much is left for us to address beyond this present analysis. Consequently, our effort here has been synoptic, and designed in large part to expose parents, teachers, and students to some of the more provocative popular literature dealing with testing and its role in American education.

Common Core State Standards (CCSS) is the name given to the current federally driven Education Standards in place for most public schools. Prior to Common Core, each state designed its own standards for teaching, essentially establishing what ought to be taught and learned at each grade level. Students would be tested by the local district and state at the end of that grade level. Teachers, students, and parents could at that point determine whether a student was on target; a measurement at least could be produced to show where each student ranked: proficient, basic, below basic, or far below basic.

An obvious problem arose: trying to compare the state scores in New York, for instance, to state scores in Mississippi. The objectivity of the scores would become virtually meaningless if each state set its own standards and tested them only in that state. For example, *what if* New York had rigorous learning expectations while Mississippi's expectations for the same grade levels were more relaxed? Theoretically, students in Mississippi might score higher and thus *appear* more advanced than the same New York students at that grade level, when in fact the reality is that the students were not only taking different tests, but tests at varying degrees of rigor. The disparity is manifestly obvious, and therefore it didn't take long for the idea to bubble to the surface that if all states had the same standards and took the *same assessment*, "true" comparisons could be made. The fallacy regarding testing and student intelligence or college readiness will be addressed in the main text, but for the sake of setting up the need for Common Core, we will proceed onward.

A natural reluctance has generally existed in each of the individual states toward submitting entirely to federalized standards and assessment, a resistance entrenched through two-hundred-plus years of states' rights to determine certain directions for themselves by their own voters. Consider how a transplant from California might find that life in Arkansas is driven by quite different values, morals, religious ideologies, etc. Consider how that difference will naturally be reflected in the local school district which chooses to emphasize certain distinctive ideas reflecting their identity in the curriculum. We are all aware of battles in certain states over Creationism vs. Evolution, and it is only the tip of the education iceberg when considered on a state-by-state basis. This state pride and local sense of identity is a very real and important facet in American life, as anyone who has traveled or met someone from another state knows. How such identity is reflected in each state is also revealed in how each state has set peculiar standards to credential its teachers, establish its own curriculum, and set the goals that the state wants for its future citizens who will be voting-age workers at the completion of their public school education. In Washington D.C. it might be simple politics, but in small-town USA, education is tied to the soil and its local citizens.

Turning over the final decision about State Education Standards to Washington D.C. might appear to the elected representatives as a fair solution to the "comparison" dilemma, but only so long as all agree that the minds and souls of those working in our capital are a fair reflection of the wills and minds of the people spread out across these fifty unique states making up the Union. However, any general election voting demographic will reveal that there are red and blue and purple states, with more and more independent or non-voting members within those states. Thus, to convince this patchwork quilt of states to fully authorize our federal government and the Congress, President, and Supreme Court with such power to determine the educational standards for all states took more than a few years and a lot of convincing—convincing in the way of billions of dollars. The carrot held in front of the states sounded too good to be true but altogether necessary to take the textbook, pencil-and-paper, antiquated school of America into the advanced age of technology-driven education.

If the obvious state differences hold true, how much money would be required to turn the heads the other way?

> The study by Accountability Works, the Maryland-based nonprofit education advocacy group, estimated that schools nationwide will need $6.87 billion for technology, $5.26 billion for professional development, $2.47 billion for textbooks and $1.24 billion for assessment testing over the first seven years that Common Core is in effect.

Where would the money come from? In 2014, the *Washington Post* revealed that the key donor(s) behind the initial funding to persuade the states to jump on board the Common Core bandwagon were Bill and Melinda Gates, i.e., the Gates Foundation. Between 2009 and 2014, over 200 million dollars was distributed by the Bill and Melinda Gates Foundation as a means to grease the wheels of change.[3] While no one can accuse Mr. or Mrs. Gates of conspiracy to

---

3   www.motherjones.com/politics/2014/09/bill-melinda-gates-foundation-common-core

write the new Common Core State Standards, it is an inescapable fact that big business and technology joined forces to convince forty-five states with the District of Columbia to sign up for the change. Where has the money gone? According to the latest reports following funds distribution, *the majority of the state money has been distributed in educational technology and software companies such as Pearson and McGraw-Hill who have profited by the hundreds of millions.* So is this really about education? Or merely profits?

But what harm is in Common Core State Standards if the teaching and testing playing board is now fairly balanced between the states? What exactly is within the Common Core Standards that makes their implementation questionable if not dangerous, other than the obvious fact that implementation has turned out to be hugely expensive for the states? *To put this point once again: the "Standards" are a red herring in this larger education problem. A cursory or critical reading of the Standards does not reveal any great shift in what ought to be taught or learned at each grade level.* For many teachers, the Common Core Standards are far less demanding than the previously required State Standards. The Standards do *not* dictate *curriculum* for the states, districts, or teachers to use. In fact, there no longer is a mandated curriculum nor textbook in many states or their respective districts. (Why bother with *more expenses?*) There is, however, an expectation that the participating states will test the students who have been taught in alignment with the Common Core Standards and such results will be made available for Washington, D.C. to evaluate and recommend future steps for each state based on the results of students' testing outcomes in those states. *This* is the fly in the ointment and where the observant and suspicious parent or teacher will take notice, namely that there is a set of Standards *without a curriculum*, followed by a final Assessment (i.e. "test") which will be reported back to the federal government.

But reported *how?*

*The fact that the test is an individually adaptive test, required to be taken by students in participating Common Core states, leads us to the greatest curiosity and implication of all, because this individually adaptive testing process, from kindergarten to the twelfth grade, is not, **nor will it be**, available in any standard printed format for the states, districts, teachers, parents, or students to consider. It is not so much a **secret** as **an impossibility** because the test is taken on a computer and makes continual personalized adjustments for the student taking the test. In other words, the test itself acts as its own artificial intelligence assessor in determining what to supply as the next question.* Imagine the teacher attempting to follow basic Standards and then having the students sit for an "individually adaptive" examination for which neither the teacher nor the student know if they have been adequately prepared. In general, the point of curriculum is to lead step by step from point A to point Z in such a systematic fashion that the student can be "objectively tested" on known material that has been taught toward the end goal—i.e., when this unit of study is over, you will be able to do or know "X." The "X" factor in this is that there is no curriculum associated to Common Core nor its final (vague and veiled) test, and so whether the arrow hits the mark is more about blind chance than aim. In this one encounters once again the "designed-in failure" of the system, for the predictable outcome should be utter failure. That must lead back to the question: why set up a system whose outcome is a guaranteed failure? We suggest one possibility, namely to open the door to the obvious "fix": a federal *curriculum* aligned to the Standards.

Who benefits from such a model? We suggest the following, though it is by no means a complete list:

1) Large technology companies who are the driving force in designing the software for new and desperately needed curriculum in the schools;

2) States that are interested in saving vast amounts of money in teacher pay and benefits, since online education does not require building new schools or classrooms nor the expense of full-time paid teachers. An adjunct teacher or proctor can be available if necessary for the unforeseen hitch in the system being down, but the curriculum, classes, assignments, tests, and e-reward gold stars do not require any new expenses that have not already been paid for by federal money utilized by students in "traditional" classrooms. As more and more online curriculum becomes the norm in order to lead toward higher scores in the online testing, "teachers" are an unnecessary financial burden and in all practical terms will be proctors and nothing more. If the unions only understood that their proclamations of more money for more technology and sharing in Common Core funding would lead to the demise of the unions and the end of teachers who "teach," they might have protected their own future as well as guaranteed human teaching for human students!

3) Some will argue (and be called conspiracy theorists) that the greatest benefit is for the "elite" who will have all the available and untraceable means toward manipulating the minds and vocational future direction of children and youth. Social reconstruction can easily take place by elevat-

ing one group, holding back another, dumbing down the entire mass of future students, indoctrination and ultimately servitude by twelve years of a single system of mental formation void of human interaction in the process of education.

Naturally this returns us to the question of funding for Common Core testing and related materials. Remember, the majority of the federal money distributed to states *has gone toward software and testing.* The numbers and names associated with the money are as follows: Apollo Global Management-owned McGraw-Hill ($72.5 million from Smarter Balanced); U.K.-based Pearson ($63 million from PARCC), and nonprofit Educational Testing Services ($42 million combined from both groups); this according to *Education Week.*

Notice carefully how the implementation of an educational ideology sparked by the fundraising of the Gates Foundation for "the good of American education" leads toward more business, a test without a trace, standards with a camel nose in the tent of "online curriculum" with all its dangers of the absence of hard-copy canonical texts, and to "electronic" texts easily adjustable to the political and corporate whims of the moment, and one begins to understand why Common Core State Standards has more than a small chance of changing everything that was once the foundation of American and, for that matter, of Western traditions of education.

We believe all of this to be under assault by the assessment process of the Common Core, and we believe that assault to be by deliberate design.

Such an agenda could only have been hatched by corporate greed, an out-of-control intelligence community, and financial and education oligarchies that have lost their own humanity and sense of moral responsibility in their endless quest for the expansion of power through the management of the grand collectivist abstractions: "the people," "the children," "the future," "democracy," "the government," and so on.

In discussing this complex interlocking network of foundations, professional groups, government agencies, testing services and corporations, we confront the fact that modern American political and cultural life is no longer that of a democratic republic, but that of a plutocracy and oligarchy. This complex interlocking network and policies, as they manifest themselves within discussions on education, we refer to in these pages simply as the "edugarchy," the educational oligarchy.

In such a short work as this, a comprehensive review of educational literature and critiques of Common Core and its predecessor policies is simply impossible. We have aimed, rather, at a high historical and philosophical overview and critique, and accordingly, have drawn from sources that we both highly recommend for their enjoyable, sometimes humorous, and always thought-provoking nature. We have tried, similarly, to draw from sources critical of the whole progressive impulse within American education that come from both a general right and left political and cultural orientation. Our goal is to stimulate not only discussion of Common Core's radical agenda for the consolidation of the surveillance state, but for its ultimate rejection.

We do this because it is ultimately an inhuman agenda, put forward by people who are ultimately inhuman, whose only cosmology, cultural aesthetic, and purpose are the stunted ones of materialism, the hive, the collective, and the machine, and the busy-ness of endless "assessment," measurement, testing, and sorting.

Joseph P. Farrell and Gary Lawrence
From somewhere, 2015

Rotten to the (Common) Core

Part One:
The Historical Matrix of the Public School and the Standardized Test

Measurement Mania
Or, Tales from the Dark Side:
Measuring the Measures and Measurers

"It is time we squarely faced the fact that institutional schoolteaching is destructive to children. Nobody survives the seven-lesson curriculum completely unscathed, not even the instructors. The method is deeply and profoundly anti-educational. No tinkering will fix it."

—

JOHN TAYLOR GATTO[1]

Consider the following list (and it's by no means complete or in any particular order): Socrates, Plato, Aristotle, Thomas Aquinas, Sir Isaac Newton, Gottfried Leibniz, Rene Descartes, Leonardo Da Vinci, Jean Calvin, Fanny Mendelssohn, Immanuel Kant, Michael Faraday, Martin Luther, Wolfgang Amadeus Mozart, Dr. John Dee, Georg Friedrich Händel, Sir Edward Coke, Augustine of Hippo, Domenico Scarlatti, Diego Velasquez, Gregory of Nazianzus, Nicholas Poussin, Giuseppi Verdi, James Clark Maxwell, Nikola Tesla, František Kupka, William Shakespeare (or, if you prefer, Edward De Vere), Francis Bacon, Marie Curie, Lise Meitner, Percy Shelley, Johann Goethe, Albert Einstein, Feodor Dostoyevsky, Peter Tchaikovsky, Clara Schumann, Franz Schubert, Ayn Rand, Johann Sebastian Bach, Adam Smith, Dante Alighieri, John Locke...

1   John Taylor Gatto, *Dumbing Us Down: The Hidden Curriculum of Compulsory Schooling* (Gabriola Island, British Columbia: New Society Publishers, 2005), pp. 17–18.

...obviously, this list could go on and on. Some of the names may be unfamiliar, some more obvious, but they all had a few things in common.

None of them attended a twentieth- or twenty-first-century American public school or university.

None of them was taught by a teacher that had to obtain a teaching "credential" at an accredited—that is to say, officially "approved"—state or private school. Indeed, some of them positively *bucked* the modern system by having been "homeschooled" by persons running small "schools" out of their homes.

None of them sat in a classroom for fifty minutes "learning" algebra from said state-credentialed instructors before being whisked away by the sound of a bell like Pavlov's dogs to sit in a class of "social studies" for another fifty minutes, to be whisked away again to *another* class of some other subject by the sound of another Pavlovian bell. As the famous (and very frustrated) American teacher John Taylor Gatto put it, "Indeed, the lesson of bells is that no work is worth finishing, so why care too deeply about anything? ... Bells inoculate each undertaking with indifference."[2]

None of the people on our list took the SAT, ACT, GRE, LSAT, Iowa Tests of Basic Skills, or any other American multiple-choice standardized test scored by computers (or, as we shall see eventually, warehouses of temporary employees of testing corporations hired to score those tests).

And all of them contributed something to the formation of Western culture, to the evolution of its science, its perceptions and philosophy of beauty, social organization, philosophy of government and institutions, its literature, art, and music. All of them were very much *individuals*, with unique views, perceptions, and genius.

To that list we might have added other names: Thomas Jefferson, Benjamin Franklin, John Adams, Alexander Hamilton, James Madison. These, too, were "highly individualized" individuals who contributed to the very founding of the United States of America and who labored to produce its Constitution of 1789.

None of *them* was taught in the modern American public school by state-certified teachers who take as many classes in "education" and "methodology" as they do in the subjects they are certified to teach.

To reiterate, *none* of them ever took the ACT, SAT, or any other standardized test that has become the staple of American schooling.

The standardized test has become such a hallmark of the system that

2   John Taylor Gatto, *Dumbing Us Down*, p. 6.

it is almost as symbolic of American public schooling as that system's dys-functional mediocrity itself. While one might point to many names of people who *have* gone through that hellish experience of modern American public schooling, to emerge either as influences on Western culture and civilization, or as pillars of symbolic brilliance in their disciplines, the historical record contra-indicates that the gimmickry and sophistry of the public schooling system, with its certifications and batteries of standardized tests, contributed anything whatsoever to their achievement and influence. The historical record indicates that, if anything, the implicit collectivist impulse in standardized testing stands in stark contrast to the basic values of individual genius and responsibility that formed the central core of the founding of the republic itself. And if anything, the success of modern products of that system of edu-cation and their achievement stands more as a warning that somewhere along the way the notions of assessment and testing (or measurement), as well as the notions of education and schooling, became confused, and that mechanistic processes were substituted for human ones. Indeed, we argue that the notion of standardized testing in general, and the Common Core assessment process in particular, are not merely symbols of systemic mediocrity in schooling, but to some extent the *ex opere operato* causes of it. We believe that this is by deliberate design, and shall so argue in the coming chapters.

Erected as it was by a few with the wealth, power, and influence to do so, this system has also resulted in the phenomenon of the "subversive teacher or professor" and the equally "subversive student," that is to say, it has led to those teachers who knowingly and personally adopt the attitude that they will teach to the best of their ability in direct competition and contradiction to what "the system" or "test rubric" dictates, and to the student that knows he or she has been shortchanged by the system, and deliberately seeks out such teachers. In this circumstance, the real teaching more often than not occurs in those quick individual exchanges of the few minutes of conversation between student and teacher after one Pavlovian bell has rung and before the next one rings. It occurs in those "subversive conversations" when the teacher confides to a student that, yes, what they say publicly in the class is to prepare them for the next standardized test, and that yes, the little clues and details that are seemingly contrary to the requirements of the next upcoming standardized test were dropped knowingly into a lecture or lesson plan; they were deliberately and with full conscious intention subversively planted, and that, yes, the student was correct to perceive that the teacher's real agenda was to see that student be the very best that he or she can be *as an individual*, and not become merely a homogenized statistic on a standardized test score. We, your authors, have both had such conversations "off the record" with our students and willingly welcomed them, and we suspect many of our readers who are teachers have had such conversations as well. The real education, and the real subversion, begins to occur when the student begins to question the whole basis, philosophy, and history of those standard tests to which he or she is so often subjected.

Well might they question them, and well that they, their parents, and society at large, *should* question them, for those tests have become the implicit sorting mechanisms that determine their future. Those tests are the dirty secret, never openly voiced, that America has not only become a massive sur-veillance-sorting state, but that the surveillance and sorting begin at an early age, in those supposedly scientific tests and measures and the corporations that create and score them.

We could put the point about modern American schooling in the form of a multiple-choice question, such as might appear on one of its multiple-choice, fill-in-the-oval-with-your-number-two-lead-pencil standardized tests:

(1) What is the solution to the problem in modern public school education?

- ⬭ A) Additional school hours
- ⬭ B) Additional weeks in the school year
- ⬭ C) Additional standardized tests given each academic year
- ⬭ D) All of the above.

If only finding a solution to the problems in modern public schooling were as easy as penciling in A, B, C, or D on a computer scan answer docu-ment! Undoubtedly, this multiple-choice guessing-game approach to solving problems in modern schooling would be ridiculed as a joke among educators. Imagine a committee taking such a test or survey to solve the problem of failing students, declining scores, and incompetence in the classroom, and waiting for a computer or senior test administrator to "calibrate the best answer" and implement the solution for all schools, students, and teachers.

An approach as previously described to solve the many problems in public schooling would be viewed as incompetent and short-sighted at best. The only modern redeeming quality would be the "collaborative" approach, the collectivist gathering, the herd decision driven to its preordained conclu-sion by the "team leader." "Experts" in the field of education worship at the throne of collaboration and sacrifice independence of thought on the altar of social architecture, draped by the tattered flag of progress (or should we say, regress?).

In order to truly comprehend the educational dialectic related to how formal "assessments" drive instruction in the classroom, one would have to begin by enduring the educational credentialing program which prepares and "qualifies" the classroom teacher. The next feat, the ring of fire in this assigned role, would be to put on a smile and attempt to maintain a positive state of mind while attending the mandatory hours of "professional development" where the *previously* taught methods in credential classes (which of course were the latest and greatest discoveries when they were taught) have now been refitted with "the most recent breakthrough methods" replacing the previously once thought of latest and greatest methods! We are reminded of a merry-go-round, lots of movement, going nowhere, or of Geoff-the-Chef at the university cafeteria, who would prepare a meal on Monday and remnants of it would be found until Fish Friday: warmed-up scrambled leftovers which were pretending to be a new dish for starving students.

Worse yet, more than a few of these "credential and professional development sessions" were as rigorous as group circles drawing on large butcher paper, followed by a presentation by each group's gender-neutral "spokesperson" who desired a spotlight to share the group's imaginative drawing with the larger audience of teachers. This was both a "learning" and "modeling" moment, one that we "could take back to the class" where the students sitting at tables could follow our example and use half a period to draw together as a means to communicate their learning. And so the vicious assessment cycle has begun its miles-long journey to collectivist feelings and sentiments.

It is precisely here that the murky rot that is at the heart of the Common Core Standards really begins, for that rottenness lies not so much in the *standards* which have been the focus of most public debate, but rather in the assessments or testing process and the credentialing process implicit in it, and in the mechanistic, materialistic, and dehumanizing assumptions implicit in both. Thus, in order to fully appreciate that rot, a look at the standardized testing industry, its origins and history, and the power elites behind it, are in order. But before we do *that*, a look at an insider's experience in the "testing busy-ness 'industry'" are in order.[3]

---

3   We simply refuse to refer to any business not directly involved in creativity and
     production as "industries"; they're not. And we simply refuse to call the corporate

A. Inside the Testing "Corporatocracy":
Whistleblower Todd Farley Talks
1. The Resemblance of Standardized Tests to Electronic Surveillance

In 2009 a remarkable book appeared: *Making the Grades: My Misadventures in the Testing Industry* by testing busy-ness insider Todd Farley. Farley, who began his career in October 1994 as a temporary worker hired to score reading tests, eventually ended as an executive for the dubiously prestigious Educational Testing Corporation in 2008.[4] During that time, Farley saw the hidden side of the testing busy-ness, from the bottom all the way to the top. In spite of having made money from the "industry," however, Farley leaves no room to doubt where he stands. Writing in his book in which he reviews his experience in copious and oftentimes simultaneously humorous and frustrating detail, Farley indicates that even though he worked in the testing business, he is unequivocally opposed to it, having seen it from within.[5] Summarizing the experiences toward the end of his book that led him to these conclusions, Farley makes an even more significant observation, one pregnant with philosophical, political, and socio-cultural implications that we explore in this book, for he had concluded that testing was not really about establishing whether a student had any real competence about the subject. The real goal, in his experience, was really merely to ensure that certain "keywords" or concepts occurred in student responses, whether or not the student actually understood their meaning.[6]

Standardized testing, in other words, resembled not so much a *test or assessment* in any real sense, but rather, an "educational" version of the National Security Agency's electronic surveillance program, where super-computers are programmed to look for the occurrence of certain keywords in certain arrangements and frequencies in email correspondence or telephone conversations. The only significant difference, in Farley's experience, was that the super-computers were replaced by human scorers to add "the human factor."

---

testing world as a "business" like banking or insurance or investing, because its track record of failure is clear. It is more appropriate to refer to the whole thing and its advocates as a "busy-ness" enjoying all the trappings of legal recognition as corporations.

4   Todd Farley, *Making the Grades: My Misadventures in the Standardized Testing Industry* (San Francisco: Berrett-Koehler Publishers, Inc.: 2009), pp. 3–4, 224.
5   Ibid., p. 223.
6   Ibid., p. 225.

As we shall eventually see, this human factor will be largely scaled down if not altogether hidden—note we say *hidden* and not *removed*—from the Common Core's individually adaptive "assessment" process.

2. The Human Factor: The Scorers Themselves

However, Farley also dispels any temptation to view this "human factor" in the scoring process that he observed and participated in as a good thing. It is, in fact, quite the opposite; it is, rather, the darky and murky truth hidden at the heart of the business, and its "temporary employees" and "hires" were more often than not individuals who could not find gainful employment anywhere else.[7] But this was not the only observation concerning the hired temporary employee-scorers Farley encountered.

One such scorer from Farley's first years in the test-scoring part of the busy-ness was "Marvin," an alcoholic who arrived every morning for work pallid and uncontrollably shaking.[8] By lunchtime, after "Marvin" had a chance to run to his car and "drink his lunch," he began to "come around," with the color returning to his face.[9] By the end of the day and several trips to his car, "Marvin" had become animated and rejoined humanity, an example of a remarkable transmutation into a functioning human being, once the alcohol craving had been satisfied, a transmutation that all the other workers, including apparently the supervisors and "professional team leaders," overlooked, lest it raise the uncomfortable questions about his performance in assessing tests![10]

This is not even the worst example recounted by Farley. Another temporary scorer was an individual who scored every paper with a "2," that is to say, a temporary scorer who scored hundreds, if not over a thousand, papers per day, and who gave each and every one a 2—but when confronted with that fact by the supervisor who discovered it, the individual in question was apparently not even the slightest bit bothered by it.[11] But wait, it gets worse, because for that day, this particular 2-obsessed individual managed to have a completely

---

7 Todd Farley, *Making the Grades*, p. 227.
8 Ibid., p. 221.
9 Ibid.
10 Ibid.
11 Ibid., p. 222.

acceptable statistical correlation[12] when his numbers were crunched by the statisticians (we'll get to *them* shortly).

But the devil, as the old saying goes, is in the details, and here we will spend some time reviewing Farley's own accounts of those devilish details, because for anyone *not* involved in testing, or the education profession, the sheer scale of the goofiness, venality, pettifoggery, silliness, sheer frustration and the endless meetings, discussions, clarifications, and other colossal wastes of time accompanying them cannot be adequately conveyed to those who have *not* lived through them except by those who, like Farley, *have* done so.

B. Farley's Details of the Testing Devil
1. Getting the Feet Wet: Farley's First Test Scoring Experience

Farley was involved not in the scoring of the computerized multiple-choice tests that most of us are familiar with, those tests we all remember from school where were told to take our number two lead pencils and blacken in the ovals, taking care to "fill them completely" but "not go outside the lines." Rather, he was involved in scoring *writing* examinations where students had either to draw or write creatively to demonstrate knowledge of a certain body of facts, and then enter a numerical score into a computer database for each paper and student, according to certain pre-established guidelines, or "rubrics."[13]

It is here that the fun and frustration—and the implications for the Common Core Assessment process—begin.

Farley's misgivings about the whole busy-ness of standardized testing and the "industry" that services it began in 1994, when a friend told him about a part-time job opportunity scoring tests for National Computer Systems, or NCS, a testing company based in Iowa City, Iowa.[14] Farley, along with other

---

12   Ibid.

13   We find it interesting that the term "rubric" should be applied as a technical term for what otherwise are simply scoring guidelines. A rubric is an instructional note in a missal or other book of ritual in Christian churches, and printed often in red ink. Such directions ensured conformity and consistency in ritual practice. Its use in the testing busy-ness might thus indicate not only a desire for consistency, but also for conformity in the practice of a ritual. It might indicate blind accepting faith in the efficacy—in this case, the "scientific" efficacy—of that ritual.

14   Todd Farley, *Making the Grades*, p. 3.

temporary scorer-employees of NCS, met for their "training" and to begin work scoring papers in a shopping mall's basement.[15] Their assignment was to score thousands of writing tests of fourth graders from a Gulf state. Farley's particular team consisted of twelve people, and their table-team leader "Anita" who would enter their scores on computers.[16]

But first, the team had to be "trained," or, to employ the pseudo-scientific jargon of the testing business, "calibrated."

Anita proceeded to explain to the team that the assignment that the nine- and ten-year-old fourth-graders had to complete was to draw a bicycle safety poster. In this case, the rubric for scoring the test was apparently very clear. If the drawn poster displayed a clear example of safety rules such as stopping at stop signs or steering the bicycle with both hands,[17] then the rubric stipulated they were to be given full credit, and a score of "1" entered on the computer for that student. On the other hand, if the poster drawing showed clear failure to understand bicycle safety such as riding with the eyes closed or with neither hand on the handle bar,[18] then no credit would be given and a score of "0" would be entered for that on the computer. Farley quips that such "rubrics" certainly made the scientific basis of standardized testing self-evident, observing that the No Child Left Behind Act refers to the practice over a hundred times.[19] It was all crystal-clear and self-evident. A bunch of fourth-grade Southern students' posters would be scored by a group of temporary employees who were "mostly white, Midwestern adults"[20] who had no direct knowledge or connection with those students.

It was simple, right?

Wrong.

On turning to his very *first* poster after this crystal-clear training—his very *first* brush at the innate ambiguities in scoring—Farley came face to face with a poster where the student had drawn himself on a bicycle, smiling the broad happy smile that children draw in their drawings, helmet firmly and clearly on his head. The only trouble was, the student was also on a flying bicycle in a huge arcing leap over what appeared to have been some sort of canal filled with flames of burning oil (or whatever), with his arms happily waving in the

15 Ibid.
16 Ibid., p. 4.
17 Ibid., p. 5.
18 Ibid.
19 Ibid., p. 6.
20 Ibid., p. 4.

unrestrained fun that children have when they're leaping their bicycles over flaming canals while wearing their helmets.

And, to underscore the safety point of the exercise, the student had cheerfully added a caption to the poster reminding people that they should wear their helmet.[21] In other words, the poster was ambiguous, and Farley turned to the "rubrics" to see a way through the ambiguity, but could not find any. Seeing his frustration, team leader Anita assured him that the poster should be scored with a "1" because the state's Department of Education had clearly stated—in its indispensable rubrics—that merely showing one safety rule earned full credit for the test, and therefore, the student was to be given full credit, without regard to the context in which it occurred.[22]

Never mind the fact that the student was jumping his bicycle across a canal of flames and apparently having a good time doing it. Never mind that no effort was extended to understand whatever process of creativity that had led the student to draw such a poster, with what may have been intended as a very tongue-in-cheek commentary: what good will a helmet do you if you're jumping your bicycle over a canal of flames? Or was the student *particularly* bright and in his own clever way trying to say "empirical exception and context always trump theoretical rubrics"?

There were inevitably ambiguities that even the wise and sage team leader Anita could not sort out. On one such occasion, Anita challenged Farley's score of a "0" because he did not see any bicycle safety rule in evidence. The reason? The bicycle was stopped behind a truck, which was in turn stopped at a stop sign. But, Anita countered to Farley, *behind* the truck there was clearly a bicycle. Farley had to argue his case, and the ensuing fun began as Farley pointed out that the bicycle, devoid of any rider at all, hardly fulfilled the "rubrics" and that it was more likely a safe car-driving rule than a bicycle one, with the All-Wise Team Leader Anita assuring him that, once again, context notwithstanding, it fulfilled the rubric. At this juncture one of the other temporary scorers joined the discussion with what would probably seem to most of us to be the relevant point, by noting that, indeed, the bicycle was completely devoid of any rider, and, besides, it was not a bicycle at a stop sign, but a truck *towing* a riderless bicycle. None of this mattered to Anita, who insisted that all her "team" could do is apply, without thought or question, the rubrics the state had promulgated.[23]

---

21 Ibid.
22 Ibid., p. 7.
23 Todd Farley, *Making the Grades*, p. 11, emphasis added.

It's probably difficult for most readers to wrap their minds around such noodle-baking nonsense—much less the fact that adults are actually wasting time debating such things—but we as your authors, having been both involved in education professionally, can assure you such mind-numbing silliness goes on all the time, and *usually if not always* when any state education "administrator," the dreaded corporate testing facilitator—the *commissar*—shows up.

Note something highly significant about Farley's story, and it's a theme we will encounter repeatedly in this book:

1) "Anita"—Farley has changed the names to protect the guilty co-conspirators in the testing busy-ness—represents the bureaucrat (whether state or corporate does not really matter). She's there to see that x amount of posters get scored in y amount of time, and hence, having to stop to debate ambiguities of common-sense commonplaces is simply out of the question. She, and those like her are, as we suggested, *commissars* whose sole mission is to ensure that "tests" are "assessed" as smoothly, quickly, and efficiently as possible. And the only way to do that is to...

2) ... adhere to the plain literal sense of the state *rubric* to the exclusion of *all* other factors, no matter how ludicrous a result that approach issues in. Anita, in short, is a *collectivist* and a *statist* bureaucrat. Once again, she, and those like her, is a commissar.

3) Thus, the scoring of the posters has nothing whatsoever really to do with the process of reasoning behind why each student drew what he or she drew, and thus, cannot truly determine if the student really understood the assignment at all. The rubricists and scorers are all disconnected from any real human contact with the student. They are mechanism, and the student is organism, and more importantly, an *individual*. It's a score, a number indicating nothing more than that a ritual process has been completed and a "rubric" fulfilled. The boy jumping his bicycle over a flaming canal is given credit because he's wearing his helmet, the empty bicycle at a stop sign chained to a flatbed truck is given credit: the rubric has been fulfilled; the mass is ended, go in peace.

But Farley was just getting *started*...

2. "The Committee Said..." : The Banality of Edubabble
a. "Calibrating the Group"

What about those "rubrics" by which the scorers are to measure and enter a numerical score on their computers? "Rubrics" on such tests are, in effect, the "canon" or "accepted paradigm" of interpretation written by "experts" on "education," and hence, for assessments of this type of test, the foundation upon which the claim to "scientific objectivity" and "validity" is grounded.[24] Consequently, when a group of temporary employees first show up to begin scoring such student papers, the first thing that occurs is that the trainer reviews the rubric for that assignment, using examples or "anchor papers" to show how the rubric was applied to derive the numerical score, a process somewhat dubiously called "calibrating" the team of scorers.[25]

Once again, the noodle-baking nonsense began almost immediately, as apparently some people in another of Farley's groups, being trained this time by "Maria," had their dials "calibrated" somewhat differently than the educational "experts" who composed the rubric, as some team members argued that selected "qualifying papers" scored with a "4" were merely "adequate," while others, of apparently less quality, were scored higher, according to the State Education experts. Debate quickly broke down into team leader Maria insistently maintaining that words like "nonetheless," "succinctly," and "beforehand" were just as good words as "alacrity," "perspicacious," and "audacity." The nonsense having become evident to Maria's "team members," one young man in his early 20s, according to Farley, saw the inevitable reduction of the logic: if qualities were to be assigned numerical quantity, then the best thing to do, to make it more "scientific," would be to assign such a value to all words, and then take some sort of average for their occurrence in a "qualifying paper" to assign a numerical score to the paper; all the words in the dictionary should be scored to indicate if they were 4s or 5s, and to determine which word choice was better than the others. Is "fastidious" better than "neatness"? "Sluggish" better than "lazy"?[26] With luck, the process might be extended to all the arts: a number value could be assigned to Bach, Chopin, Glenn Miller, and Duke Ellington, to compare their relative artistic and musical merit.

---

24 Todd Farley, *Making the Grades*, p. 189.
25 Ibid., p. 53.
26 Todd Farley, *Making the Grades*, pp. 46–47.

Absurd? Of course it is.

However, notice two significant things in this little exchange. Firstly, for "Maria" as for "Anita," the ultimate authority was some far-removed rubrics committee, a "Supreme Soviet of Literary Merit," whose diktats were final. Conformity to this Soviet, and its decisions, was the real criterion of an authentic and hence "valid" score. Her role in "calibrating the group" was, in other words, to *"decalibrate" individual evaluations* and institute in its place a "group consensus" adherent to the committee. This will become a crucial point when we turn to the Common Core assessment process. What the process was ultimately geared to do was not to produce genuine insight on the part of the scorer, but rather, to produce conformity, consensus, and above all, an absolute obedience to collective groupthink.[27] The second point to notice is that the "rubricists," the people composing the scoring guidelines of the rubrics, remain, for the scorers and for the students being scored, utterly anonymous, as do *the processes of reasoning behind the establishment of their scoring guidelines.* And let us be blunt: the fact that they think a set of "rubrics" can be designed to account for all types of individual human thought processes and creativity is just as silly as a boy in his helmet jumping his bicycle over a canal of flames. Indeed, it is even sillier, and we can thank Farley, and the boy, for pointing it out.

At this juncture, the utterly subjective basis of scoring such papers should be evident, a point illustrated by one of "Maria's" gaffes as she sought to "range-find" and "calibrate the group." Again, the mind-baking devil is in the details, for while "calibrating" yet another group, the inevitable discussion broke out on why an "anchor paper," scored a "4" and not a "3" by the "State Range-Finding Committee" (no kidding folks, that's what it was called), was scored that way in the first place. After adamantly defending the wisdom of the State Range-Finding Committee for several minutes to a group of perplexed scorers, Maria's assistant, "Ricky," slithered over to her bearing a paper, and hissed something into Maria's ear.

Glances were exchanged. The paper was peered at. Maria, now slumping, sighed, looked up to Heaven (perhaps with that "why me?" look on her face), then finally executed a *volte-face* pirouette, confronted the group to which she had been defending the *ex cathedra* pronouncements of the State Range-Finding Soviet, apologized, and admitted that she had made a mistake: the paper was not a 4, but a 3.[28]

---

27 Todd Farley, *Making the Grades,* pp. 36–37.

28 Todd Farley, *Making the Grades,* p. 49, italics and bold emphasis added.

All hail the State Range-Finding Soviet.

And remember, while you're singing the praises of the State Range-Finding Soviet and the wonders of scientific standardized tests, that these tests, *by law*, are being used to make determinations on which schools, which faculties, which individual teachers, which principals, and above all, which students are "succeeding" and which are "failing."[29] Remember this point, for it will become *very* significant when we finally turn to consider the Common Core assessment process. And again, we can assure you, Farley's experiences dovetail almost perfectly with our own encounters with education commissars.

But in the meantime, if you thought it couldn't *possibly* become any goofier, you'd be very wrong. Consider first the case of...

b. ... The Correct Adjective for the Flavor of Pizza (and Ice Cream)

Eventually Farley worked his way up to become a "table leader," overseeing a small team gathered at one table and scoring student papers describing their favorite food, and being assigned a number for the use of vocabulary words. You can imagine the banal fun that ensued when Farley was asked for the "correct" adjective to describe the flavor of "pizza." "Salty," "sweet," "bitter" were all soon flying in conversation in a blizzard of confusion, with each proposed "acceptable" term hotly contested by various members of the "calibrated group" as individuals quickly pointed out that the "answer" depended on the type of pizza in question, and whether it had anchovies, pineapples, various types of cheeses...[30]

You can guess the rest, as these grown adults had to stop to reach a "command decision" and "consensus of the Pizza Soviet" on how to score papers on the flavor of pizza, a discussion which soon turned to ice cream and whether or not to accept the adjective "salty." Here, Farley's command decision to accept only "sweet" was overridden when someone pointed out that one student, who had described ice cream as "salty," might have been referring to pistachio ice cream.[31]

---

29 Ibid., p. 81.
30 Todd Farley, *Making the Grades*, pp. 125–126.
31 Ibid., p. 127.

c. Determining the Rubric: Was that "Fizzes" or "Fizzles"?

Eventually, Farley climbed all the way up the testing ladder to land a cushy position at one of the largest and best-known testing corporations in America, the Educational Testing Service in Princeton, New Jersey. Using this to further his career, he quit this job and became a testing consultant. During one of these consultancies, Farley had the chance to sit in on a conference call between experts from the Educational Testing Service and another testing corporation, Pearson.[32] On this occasion, the conference call was a group of "disembodied voices" deciding on the standards that would eventually become part of a chemistry paper "rubric." The call was moderated by one "Olivia," the liaison and coordinator from the Educational Testing Service. The conversation that Farley recounts is a rare glimpse into the "scientific" nature of rubrics and standardized tests, and well worth the read, as grown adults in a conference call debate the relative merits of answers to describe a chemical reaction. Does it sizzle? Boil? Foam? Fizz? Fizzle? Bubble?[33]

The numbing banality of this conversation exposes not only the faulty "science" behind rubrics for scoring essays, it exposes "rubric creep" itself, as some sort of on-the-spot groupthink consensus has to be engineered over every pettifogging detail, to eliminate the *human* factor of discernment to make it "scientific."

It can have serious consequences, as Farley recounts an incident where, one year, a trainer of a group evaluating science essays issued the ukase that "recycling" would *not* be accepted as a response for a way to reduce atmospheric carbon dioxide, because the process consumed too much energy. The *next* year's trainer decided to *accept* that response.[34] So an important question occurs: how did each decision affect the statistics on that question over the span of years it occurred on the test? On another occasion, Farley observed a trainer telling "his scorers to give full credit to the idea a wildlife expert was 'observing,' 'watching,' 'following,' or 'tracking' a herd of elephants, but only partial credit to the idea he was 'studying' them."[35] In other words, *any question* can change from year to year, depending on which trainer decides which are acceptable responses, to be given full credit according to a "rubric," and which are not. So how reliable are the "reliability numbers" of the stan-

---

32 Ibid., p. 160.

33 Todd Farley, *Making the Grades*, pp. 161–163.

34 Ibid., p. 196.

35 Todd Farley, *Making the Grades*, p. 197.

dardized tests? How reliable is the statistical average over the years, not only on specific questions but on the tests themselves?

3. The Unreliability of the Reliability Numbers

Farley recounts one incident that explodes the notion that the reliability numbers are reliable. They are everything *but*. The incident once again involved "Olivia" and a mysterious group called "the psychometricians," the statisticians compiling all the results. We'll get back to them in a moment, but first, the incident occurred in a conversation between Olivia and Farley, when Olivia realized that Farley's and her results in scoring a particular test were falling *outside* the acceptable statistical margins, because her scores and Farley's were agreeing too much! (So much for "calibrating the group.") Thus, Olivia and Farley had to get "Brian" to help rescore the papers.

Voilà! Solution found! Statistical margins achieved! They had "valid score results."[36]

In other words, when all is said and done—after the "rubric creep" and the changes from year to year in what answers some leaders will accept and what ones they will not accept—if your group is still falling outside of the statistical prediction, simply "renormalize" or *doctor* the numbers until they are acceptable!

Such quackery—such *fraud*—is perhaps best illustrated by the term used to describe the educational testing "industry's" statisticians and what they do: psychometricians and psychometry. The term is revealing, for what they are trying to do is "measure the soul," and it is perhaps even *more* revealing that this same term, psychometry, also has a paranormal or "esoteric" significance, for in those contexts it means the "subtle imprinting" of an individual's soul—its "vibrations," to use the esoteric and paranormal buzzword—on physical objects

---

36 Todd Farley, *Making the Grades*, pp. 147–148. See also Farley's encounter with "Lydia" on p. 175. For those in the state of California, where the law requires high school seniors to pass the California High School Exit Exam in order to gain their diploma, Farley, who led teams scoring these exams, states "Without getting into the specifics of it, I'd say the scoring of the CAHSEE essays was exactly as efficacious as the scoring of any other project I'd ever been associated with." (p. 149) Farley also recounts that he was paid "25 a pop" to write questions for this exam, and $500 for short stories to be included on it (p. 150), which raises another important question, *just who is writing the questions for the tests, and what are their qualifications?*

in more or less steady physical proximity to him or her. These "imprints," so the lore would have it, remain in the objects and can be "read" or "recovered" by psychics "tuned in" to them. This is the reason many psychics, when investigating crimes for police or sheriff's departments, ask for something belonging to the victim. It is curious that such a term would also be used to describe the measurement process of standardized testing, or is it? As we shall see in the next few chapters, there may have been more afoot in the origins of standardized testing than meets the eye.

4. Interpreting the Rubric, or Rubric Creep

But the psychometric quackery in the "reliability numbers" can occur in an entirely *different* way as well, beyond outright doctoring of the numbers or "renormalization" (to employ the physics term), and we have hinted at it already by pointing out how answers acceptable on a particular item one year might not be acceptable the next year, depending on who is doing the training and what instructions they give to the scorers. In one instance, Farley recounts a case where, in the *same* testing session being scored by the *same* group of temporary hires, the group leader, the irrepressible "Roseanne," changed the group consensus of the scoring of an "anchor paper" *midway through the scoring session,* a classic case of "rubric creep" or, perhaps in this instance, rubric gallop. Thus, "Per Roseanne's instructions, essays of *exactly the same ability* would get different scores based only on *when* they were read: essays that would have earned a 2 in the first half of the project would earn a 3 during the second half, and on an assessment that *mattered!*"[37] The test, and hence the scores, mattered because on this particular examination, students' futures—their ability to get scholarships, or even to enter their chosen field—were at stake. Nonetheless, the leader of the testing Soviet decided during the same testing session to alter the basis of the groupthink consensus.

The whole process of "calibrating the group" and "range-finding" and reliability numbers could be adjusted at will, if the numbers were not falling within acceptable limits, never mind the fact that people's futures were being determined by such a process of quackery.

---

37 Todd Farley, *Making the Grades*, p. 95, emphasis in the original.

5. Eliminating the Human Factor

So what do we have at the end of Mr. Farley's litany of experiences as a "testing professional"?

By now, it should be clear: whether at the stage of the *formation* of rubrics, or at the stage of interpreting and applying them, or at the stage of the formation of the standardized test questions and assignments themselves, or at the stage of scoring individual samples, or at the stage of compiling statistics, the whole process is anything *but* standardized, and is dependent upon the qualitative evaluations of humans.

The whole process could be made so much smoother, faster, and more efficient if only the human element in scoring essay and writing examinations could be removed from the equation, just like is being touted for the Common Core assessment process, right?[38]

Wrong.

If anything, the idea that statistical or scoring consistency can be obtained by turning it over to a computerized battery of *adaptive* tests only raises the stakes of the basic question: who are the people programming the computers? What are their qualifications? What are the parameters by which the program, the questions, and the evaluation system were created?

To state these questions openly may reveal what part of the hidden agenda of the Common Core assessment process may really be, for without all those temporary hires, no more stories can leak out about just how fraudulent the "industry" is; no more stories can leak out from witnesses to the process about group leaders, speaking either for the local state educational soviet, unilaterally adjusting the numbers or criteria for evaluation; no more stories can leak out about rubric creep, and additionally, those scores can now be adjusted—to "make the numbers work," or for any *other* reason one may have to hack someone's future—by a few keystrokes of anonymous "psychometricians" employed by private testing cartels feeding at the trough of government money.

The potential for mischief only *begins* here. Such standardized tests can be the perfect platform by which to build "personality profiles" and to gauge the effectiveness of various social engineering programs and to mine for other sorts of data under the guise of "educational" testing. But we're getting ahead of ourselves.

---

38 Q.v. Farley, *Making the Grades*, p. 152 where the possibility is discussed.

Just how did all this measurement mania really come about? Who was behind it? And why? Was it ever really about improving education? Or was it about something else?

Take a deep breath...

The Twitification of America
"Facilitators" and the Standardized Test

"Into this carnival of magical thinking has come a parade of profit-seekers: analysts, consultants, researchers, academic houses, writers, advisors, columnists, textbook committees, school boards, testing corporations, journalists, teachers colleges, state departments of education, monitors, coordinators, manufacturers, certified teachers and administrators, television programs, and hordes of school-related businesses—all parasitic growths of the government monopoly over the school concept."

"Monopoly schooling.... certifies permanent experts who enjoy privileges of status unwarranted by the results they produce."

—

JOHN TAYLOR GATTO[1]

T o Gatto's list of experts enumerated in the above epigrams, we might include one other, one that anyone professionally involved in teaching has encountered at one time or another. Teachers frequently suffer the psychologically damaging spiritual, emotional, and intellectual rape of an encounter with "the Facilitator," a vapid, empty, brainless twit, a person who is as deep as a puddle and whose puddle contains no water or anything else of substance, a shallow hollow into which anything can be poured. The Facilitator is the extremity of political correctness, insisting at every turn upon the gender-neutral language promoted and advocated

---

[1]   John Taylor Gatto, *Dumbing Us Down: The Hidden Curriculum of Compulsory Schooling* (Gabriola Island, British Columbia: New Society Publishers, 2005), pp. 88, 90, respectively.

by the Edugarchy. Robert/a, we'll call him/her, is a bundle of oppositions. Indeed, s/he is—to paraphrase a medieval observation wildly out of context—a bundle of accidents without substance waiting to transubstantiate into another bundle of accidents. Robert/a's "professional biography" is an orgy of narcissism, shallowness, and a veritable typhoon of verbal padding of banal, trendy-sounding groupthink claptrap signifying the annihilation of anything of substance whatsoever. We may envision her/him as also indulging in a variety of "spiritual practices" including private invocations of all the sublime and miserific powers of mediocrity and other High Evil before conducting his/her workshops, for we sense in her/his androgynous presence their draining and sapping forces hovering just around the corner of our perception, casting their shadow over the whole panoply of "the continuing education workshop."

Every teacher has encountered her/him at one time or another; s/he is the perpetually smiling education commissar whose task is to reinforce the attitudes and policies of the Edugarchy, whose sole *modus operandi* in dealing with other people is to view them as a collective or group, which in turn has to respond to his/her bells and whistles and time limits, which has to perform a variety of kindergarten "group activities" imposed by a variety of passive-aggressive techniques. Individuals who do *not* so conform are, of course, not "team players" and have "bad attitudes." Robert/a is, however, a fraud and his/her life has been a fraud, for s/he is a vastly overpaid shill for collectivization; s/he earns tens of thousands of dollars from corporate, foundation, and local, state, and federal government grants, and serves on a variety of professional association boards, in order to peddle her/his metaphysically bankrupt nonsense at the many such "required class activities" that teachers must endure to obtain their certifications. Robert/a thrives in the covens of "continuing education," and "professional training" and "leadership assessment" meetings, and teachers and managers and hence ultimately children and workers and the public and culture at large are Robert/a's primary victims. S/he thrives on self-congratulation and the flattery of her/his brainwashed victims. Robert/a is, her/himself, a product of the whole miserable process, having been subjected to it when s/he sought and gained his/her "teacher certification" or degree in "leadership." But s/he is not a victim, for s/he long ago sold her/his shriveled soul for the fleshpot of "method" and the *ersatz* culture of the artificial "group" and a blizzard of pointless activity.

Teachers will have had experience with something else as well: Robert/a reassures his/her "team" that her/his activities schedule is "flexible" and that everyone "learns in a different way" and that these "individual approaches" need to be "nurtured and respected," but on the day of his/her commissarial epiphanies, s/he deviates little if at all from her/his schedule, shuts down any genuine discussion in depth due to "time limits" (especially on topics not on his/her agenda), dismisses any real focus on content or issues of substance, subjects roomfuls of adults to childish kindergarten activities (an extreme form of passive aggression), and exhibits other forms of passive aggression against individuals who decline to participate in his/her activities according to her/his prescriptions. Both of your authors have been subjected to hours of this nonsense, both in "certification" classes and in "continuing education." Now, we realize that all this "fractionalized gender-neutral language" might be a bit hard on the eyes, and may be causing lovers of the English language to grind and gnash their teeth, but we can assure you, the edublither and political correctness that now dominate American education *are* this bad, if not much worse. But we will spare the reader any further exercises in "gender fractions." We employed it only to show how even language itself has been transformed into a tool of demonstrating conformity to an agenda dictated by the Edugarchy.

Such characterizations might seem a slightly humorous if not linguistically horrific update of the fairy tale *The Emperor's/Empress' New Clothes,* but anyone who has attended "teacher certification" or "continuing education" workshops will recognize the standard template in play in the commissar's passive-aggressive, narcissistic techniques, for while there is always a great deal of *talk* about individualism, creativity, and freedom, and reassurances that these are "respected and appreciated," this talk occurs in a context of group activity designed to counteract it by emphasizing the lowest common denominator and the group.

Those who *have* pointed out that such commissars are, like the Emperor/ Empress with her/his new clothes, not only naked but in that nakedness, deluded in the creations of their own twittery, however, have done so in a manner that challenged the whole dystopian philosophy of the credentialed facilitator gods and goddesses of "continuing education" and the juvenile mindless madness of their activities and tests.

But what do all these overpaid[2] edu-commissars have to do with standardized testing? Patience, we'll get there, but by way of some early critiques of standardized tests and a bit of history.

---

2 If they charge any more than $.01 for their "services," then in our opinion, they're overcharging.

One of those who critiqued the tests and their wider cultural implications was a friend and professional colleague of Albert Einstein, the mathematician Banesh Hoffmann,[3] and the book in which he took aim at the whole pyramid of tests and workshops and "continuing education" was his early 1960s classic *The Tyranny of Testing*, a review of his running battle with standardized tests in general, and with the Education Testing Corporation and its progenitor, the College Testing Board, in particular.

A. Hoffmann, the Standardized Test, and the Punishment of Individual Brilliance and Creativity
1. Jacques Barzun's Foreword

Hoffmann's book, first published in 1962, begins with a Foreword by Jacques Barzun, who observed that he first raised similar philosophical objections to "scientific testing" in a short article published in *The Teacher in America* in the 1940s. After the appearance of this article, Hoffmann quipped that "The most charitable view of my madness was that I was the product of a foreign school system well known to be backward and resistant to modern methods."[4] The source of Hoffmann's "madness" was his main thesis, namely, that "mechanical tests raised mediocrity above talent"[5] and that the mechanical standardized test has but "the trappings of science"[6] which, though employed "in good faith" accomplish nothing but the production of "disastrous results";[7] moreover, they not only "repress individuality," but also misread the statistics and performance that the tests gather.[8]

Barzun also notes, somewhat ironically, that in the early 1960s America appeared to be "recovering from its infatuation with fallacious 'methods' in several realms—not only in the giving of tests but also in the teaching of

---

3   Hoffmann will be familiar to readers of Joseph's book *Secrets of the Unified Field*, for Hoffmann was also a friend and associate of the brilliant Hungarian electrical engineer Gabriel Kron, and authored not only an introduction to one of Kron's books, but some articles on Kron's adaptation of tensors to electrical engineering problems.

4   Banesh Hoffmann, *The Tyranny of Testing* (Mineola, New York: Dover Books, 2003), p. 8.

5   Ibid.

6   Ibid., pp. 9–10.

7   Ibid., p. 10.

8   Ibid.

reading, in the training of teachers" and so on, while countries in Europe such as France and Germany, were rapidly "Americanizing" by adopting the same practices.[9] Sadly, Barzun was only half correct: Europe continued on the American "path," while America *also* continued to do so. Far from overcoming its infatuation with the fleshpot of "method" and standardized tests and "facilitation," Common Core has now put American education on the steroids of edubabble.

But back to Hoffmann, and Barzun's Foreword.

Barzun sums up Hoffmann's basic approach and thesis as demonstrating the two principal effects of standardized tests, for

> ...an objective test of mind is a contradiction in terms, though a fair test, a searching examination, a just *estimate*, are not. Among the tests that are unfair, certainly, are those *which penalize the finer mind—as Mr. Hoffmann proves*—and **those which, through the forceful use of wrong answers,** *may divert that mind from the accurate knowledge it possessed a moment before.*[10]

The punishment of individual brilliance and creativity, and the "forceful use of *wrong* answers" on standardized tests: these twin pillars are the basis on which Hoffmann constructs his devastating critique and exposure of the "testing busy-ness."

2. "Simple" Questions, the Problem of Interpretation, and the Punishment of "the Finer Mind"

"The crucial question," Hoffmann observes, "is with us still: *what sense is there in giving tests in which the candidate just picks answers, and is not allowed to give reasons for his choices?*"[11] The question assumes great importance given the reliance on such tests as a sorting mechanism for social engineering, for such standardized tests are the gatekeepers for admissions to colleges, universities, professional schools, grants, scholarships, corporate and military promotions.[12]

With these observations in hand, Hoffmann begins his assault on standardized testing by taking the reader through a sampling of real test questions

---

9 Banesh Hoffmann, *The Tyranny of Testing*, p. 8.

10 Ibid., pp. 10–11, all emphases added.

11 Ibid., p. 20, emphasis added.

12 Banesh Hoffmann, *The Tyranny of Testing*, pp. 20–21.

designed to illustrate how such tests, in fact, penalize the more informed test-taker, and how they in fact begin a process of inculcating the game of social and psychological "doubt," a game which both your authors, having been subjected to these tests, have been forced to play themselves!

> For example, I am told that on a certain test a question appeared of which the following is the gist:
>> *Emperor* is the name of
>> (A) a string quartet
>> (B) a piano concerto
>> (C) a violin sonata
>
> This seems to be a simple, straightforward question. The average student quickly picks answer B and proceeds untroubled to the next question, perhaps feeling elated at being given so simple a test. But what of the superior student? He knows of the *Emperor Concerto* of Beethoven, but he also knows of the *Emperor Quartet* of Haydn; and his knowledge puts him at a disadvantage, for because of it he must pause to weigh the relative merits of answers A and B while his more fortunate, less well-informed competitors rush ahead.
> In this particular case the superior student does not ponder long. Two theories occur to him: the examiner is malicious, or the examiner is ignorant of the Haydn work. ...
> .... For he has been led to call into question both the good will and the competence of the examiner.... And whenever he comes to a question for which he, with his superior ability, sees more than one reasonable answer, he must stop to evaluate afresh the degrees of malice and incompetence of the examiner.[13]

This "second-guessing" of the examiner is a game all of us who have ever taken such a test have played, for the question "What does he *want* as an answer?" is a question we have all asked ourselves before examination time. The problem here is that one is being asked to second-guess an anonymous question-writer with whom one has never come into contact, and to supply a series of answers to such questions on tests that will significantly influence the life opportunities of the individuals taking the test. The multiple-choice

---

13   Ibid., p. 23.

standardized test is thus really only a test of the test-takers' abilities to read the testers' minds, a point brought home by the fact that it is also known among test-takers as the "multiple guess" test.[14]

3. Testing the Tests

Like Farley, Hoffman reviews some of the procedures designed to convince everyone that such standardized tests are "scientific" or, to use that dreaded word, "objective," a word that takes on new meaning in the surreal world of testing, for the first stage in compiling such a "scientific" and "objective" test is for a committee to be formed, under the leadership of "an expert on test-making, usually one trained in psychology."[15] This individual "calls in consultants who are expert in the subject to be tested and other experts as they are needed."[16]

So far, so good... or is it?

Recall the critiques addressed so far with respect to some questions, namely, that the test-*taker*—particularly the more informed one—is put into the position of having to read the mind of the test-maker, which, as it turns out, is not *one* mind, but *several*. The test-taker, in other words, must guess at a *consensus* of minds, not just at *one* mind.[17] Finally, the test is "pre-tested," or to use Farley's term, "validated," as the test is given to a group of people to compile individual statistics for each question.[18] Once these statistics have been compiled, they are gathered into "a descriptive *manual* along with much other descriptive and technical matter about the test: for example, its aims, the formulas used in computing the statistics, instructions to the prospective user on how to administer the test,"[19] and so on.

But it is evident from Hoffmann's review that there is nothing whatsoever that is objective about such a test, unless "objectivity" is to be ascribed to group consensus over that of an individual, and even then, as we shall see, the group can be "objectively, factually *wrong*" whereas the individual can be

---

14 See the discussion in Banesh Hoffmann, *The Tyranny of Testing*, pp. 72–74.

15 Ibid., p. 53.

16 Ibid.

17 See Hoffmann's amusing description of the process of committee-designed questions on p. 54.

18 Banesh Hoffmann, *The Tyranny of Testing*, p. 55.

19 Ibid., p. 57.

objectively, factually *correct*. Indeed, in the final analysis, the only objective thing about such tests is the fact that no subjective, or human, element "enters the *process* of grading once the key is decided upon,"[20] a key that, again, is merely a *consensus of experts*, which is fed into a machine, which "objectively" evaluates the examinations.

In the face of such deep issues arising when he began to challenge the whole philosophical basis of standardized tests in the 1950s and 1960s, the College Entrance Examination Board, a heavy user of the Educational Testing Service's widely used Scholastic Aptitude Test, or SAT, went from *admission* in 1956, to *omission* in 1960, and here it is worth citing Hoffmann at length:

> Again, in a booklet *Scholastic Aptitude Test*, published by the College Entrance Examination Board in 1956, describing tests given to students seeking admission to college, and giving sample questions, the following advice is offered on page 18:
>
>> "As you read through the explanations of the verbal section, you may disagree with what we think to be the correct answer to one or two questions. You may think we are quibbling in making certain distinctions between answer choices. If is true that you will find some close distinctions and just as true that in making close distinctions reasonable people do disagree. Whether or not you disagree on a few questions is not terribly important, however, for the value of the test as a whole is that people who are likely to succeed in college agree in the main on most of the correct answers. It is this that gives the [Scholastic Aptitude Test] its predictive power.
>>
>> "For this reason, when you find it hard to make or recognize a distinction between answer choices, it is better not to spend much time on that question. It is the whole [Scholastic Aptitude Test] rather than any single question in it that makes the test a good indicator of college ability."[21]

Hoffmann comments as follows:

> The advice in the last paragraph quoted above has significant implications. Consider it in the light of these mutually exclusive propositions: (a) the test

---

20 Ibid., p. 61.
21 Banesh Hoffmann, *The Tyranny of Testing*, p. 74.

contains genuinely difficult questions that are free from ambiguity but call for reflection and can not [sic] be properly analyzed in a short time; and (b) the test is devoid of such questions.

If (b) is true, the advice is reasonable, but the test is unworthy of the highly gifted student since it gives him little if any chance to display his superiority over his merely clever rivals. If (a) were true, the advice would defeat the purpose for which the genuinely difficult questions were included, and would be tantamount to a plea for superficiality despite the presence of these questions. It is difficult to escape the conclusion that the two paragraphs together amount to an admission that genuine depth is not present in the test. What they seem to imply is that the difficult questions are difficult not because they have depth but because they involve close distinctions about which there is room for legitimate doubt; and one may be excused for regarding this as a euphemistic way of confessing ambiguity.

The College Entrance Examination Board seems to have regretted this possibly unintentional admission, for in the 1960 edition of the booklet *Scholastic Aptitude Test* it omits it, and says merely, "Since you will have only a limited amount of time for each section of the test, use your time effectively and work as rapidly as you can without losing accuracy...."[22]

In other words, in the face of a potential philosophical difficulty regarding the alleged "scientific and objective" nature of the Educational Testing Service's SAT, the College Entrance Examination Board simply defaulted, and whisked the difficulty away into the dustbin without ever really addressing it; like Yezhov and Yagoda in the *Soviet Encyclopedias* of the Stalin era, such difficulties were merely purged, and the photos, or in this case, the test "booklets" were simply "retouched."

This is not education; it is fraud.

B. The Real Goal?:
Hoffmann vs. The Educational Testing Service on Questions of Science
1. Deeper Ambiguities and Analogies

Hoffmann's, like Farley's, disenchantment with the world of professional testing grew, and the more he probed, the more shrill the "defense" of the "testing

---

22 Ibid., pp. 74–75, bold emphasis added.

process" became, for the testers attempted to belittle the philosophical objections "by using such terms as 'nit-picking' and by suggesting that defective questions are few and far between."[23] But unfortunately, the examples of such questions were not "few and far between," but the ever-present reality of an underlying philosophy and worldview present in the whole notion of standardized testing; "one has but to shake the tree," Hoffmann maintained, "and they fall in abundance."[24]

One such question that fell from the tree was a question that appeared on a National Merit Scholarship test, which was brought to Hoffmann's attention by a candidate who actually took the test, and sent him an example of a question that, once again, assumed no real specialized insight on the part of the test-taker:

> Through the courtesy of the test publisher, I am able to give the question he mentions exactly as it appeared on the test:
>
>> "DIRECTIONS: To mark an exercise, first decide which of the four words, if any, is incorrectly spelled. Then find the corresponding row of boxes on the answer sheet, and mark the box corresponding to the misspelled word. If none of the words is misspelled, which is often the case, mark the last box in the row.
>>
>> 98. 1) cartons
>>   2) altogether
>>   3) possibilities
>>   4) intensionally
>>   5) none wrong[25]

My correspondent wrote to me about this question as follows:

> "when I reached 'intensionally,' I frankly was stumped. While the word is a perfectly good word, **frequently used in logic and semantics**, I knew that the test was for seventh through twelfth graders; if the test-makers

---

23 Banesh Hoffmann, The Tyranny of Testing, p. 210.

24 Ibid., p. 211.

25 Hoffmann gives the source of this question as The Iowa Tests of Educational Development, Test 3, Part II, p. 9 (Form X-3S, separate booklet edition, published by Science Research Associates, Inc. Q.v. Hoffmann, The Tyranny of Testing, p. 86.

intended 'intensionally' to be counted as correct, then the question became a test of vocabulary, not spelling ability; if they intended 'intensionally' to be counted wrong, then they were denying the word a place in the English language. I marked choice 5. After the test, I found out that the key indicates that 'intensionally' is misspelled.

"Aside from the simple inaccuracy of Science Research Associates, publishers of the test, it strikes me as unfair to punish a student for knowing too much. The word 'intensionally' **is frequently used in S.I. Hayakawa's *Language in Thought and Actions*, one of the textbooks for the Special Senior English course at ... School. Most of the Special Senior English class "missed" Question 98, while the remainder correctly guessed that S.R.A. had never heard of 'intensionally.'"**[26]

In other words, the test-taker knew of a specialized terminology in semantics and logic that was *not* known by the test-makers and their committees of "experts," and was thus left in the horns of a dilemma: did he, a candidate for a National Merit Scholarship, assume the experts knew what he knew, and mark answer 5 as the correct answer, or did he assume they did not, and mark answer 4?

But either way, in the end, the observation stands: the test-makers had designed a test in which more knowledgeable takers were penalized for their knowledge, for the "correct" answer, the one sought by Science Research Associates, was indeed answer number 4, which in the final analysis, was incorrect! As Hoffmann observes in another context,

It is not without significance that the professional testers refer to the "wrong" answers as "distractors," "misleads," and "decoys." The decoys are deliberately designed to seem plausible. They are, in fact, deliberate traps.[27]

But traps for whom? In this case, for the more well-read test-taker, who had a degree of specialized knowledge beyond that of the test-makers themselves.[28]

---

26 Ibid., p. 86, boldface emphasis added.

27 Banesh Hoffmann, *The Tyranny of Testing*, p. 69.

28 Indeed, the use of such deliberate traps and decoys is similar to the technique used in some occult writings and texts of the "blind," i.e., deliberately obfuscated and ambiguous language designed to lead a non-initiate into dead ends, superficial tangents, and cul-de-sacs.

It is obvious from the nature of the tests that they do not give the candidate a significant opportunity to express himself. If he is subtle in his choice of answers it will go against him; and yet there is no other way for him to show any individuality. If he is strong-minded, non-conformist, unusual, original, or creative—as so many of the truly important people are—he must stifle his impulses, and conform as best he can to the norms that the multiple-choice testers set up in their unimaginative, scientific way. The more profoundly gifted the candidate is, the more his resentment will rise against the mental straitjacket into which the testers would force his mind. And if, by the questions they use, the testers betray intellectual incompetence, the profound student can hardly escape a feeling of contempt—contempt tinged with dismay that these are the people who have acquired the power to judge him.[29]

This is quite the crucial point, as we shall discover in the next chapter, for it raises the question of why an intellectually mediocre testing elite should want or wish to wield such power; it raises the question of what might be the real agenda or the potential but unintended implication behind such a social dichotomy, for when such tests become the sorting mechanisms and determiners of destiny that they have become with their widespread use, "The zest and creativity of a business organization may be dampened and destroyed. The strength and vitality of a nation may be jeopardized.... Professional judgment becomes overawed and atrophied, and professional testers take over."[30]

The real question is, is such atrophy and dumbing-down an unintended consequence of such educational programs and tests, or is it a deliberate component of a larger scheme of social engineering?

2. Use of Statistics by Test-Defenders

Part of the answer to that question is suggested by the strategies and tactics used to defend the tests and to deflect deeper philosophical criticism, and like Farley, Hoffmann identifies the appeal to "statistics" as being a primary component in this defensive arsenal: "Statistics are no substitute," he warns, "for

---

29 Ibid., pp. 91–92.
30 Banesh Hoffmann, *The Tyranny of Testing*, p. 103.

intellectual standards, nor are they a shield against all types of criticism."[31] Indeed, Hoffmann raises the very same philosophical objection with respect to the appeal to "statistics" that we pointed out in the previous chapter with the examples from Todd Farley's experience in the testing "business":

> If the original test favored the quick-reading, superficially brilliant, cynically test-wise candidate and penalized the intellectually honest candidate with a subtle, probing, critical, or creative mind, then subsequent versions will do just the same. **The inbred statistics gathered by the test-maker will reflect the homogenization that his procedure has imposed, but they will not reveal that what was homogenized and perpetuated was something warped. These inbred statistics will show gratifying consistency between the old and the new versions of the test, but they will not reveal the grave imperfections of the test as an instrument for selecting the best candidates, in any sense of the word "best" other than that so one-sidedly defined by the test itself.** On the contrary, the deceptive consistency of these, as of other, incestuous statistics produces a false sense of security, contentment, and scientific justification, and becomes a convenient device for stifling criticism and convincing the unwary.[32]

Or to put it "country simple":

> A person who uses statistics does not thereby automatically become a scientist, any more than a person who uses a stethoscope automatically becomes a doctor. Nor is an activity necessarily scientific just because statistics are used in it.[33]

In practice, however, the tactics of defense are more subtle, and consist of a series of steps designed less to answer criticisms than to exhaust the critic.

In words that almost directly parallel the experience of Farley, Hoffmann summarizes these "defensive belts" and the "defense-in-depth" and "exhaustion" strategy that they imply:

> The test-makers have developed a strikingly effective routine for dealing with their critics. When confronted with general criticisms that they find they

---

31 Ibid., p. 135.

32 Banesh Hoffmann, *The Tyranny of Testing*, pp. 137–138, boldface emphasis added.

33 Ibid., p. 143.

can not [sic] simply ignore, **they make a show of patient reasonableness. Of course they welcome concerned criticism, they say. But the critic is just an amateur offering mere opinion, not scientific fact. After all, they are experts, and they know.** Having said this, they go on to speak of the high professional competence of the people who make their tests. They point with pride to the elaborate scientific ritual they follow in constructing and evaluating their tests. And then, for the *coup de grâce,* they bring out their big gun—their "statistics show..." **maneuver;** by insisting that "statistics show...," they surround themselves with such an aura of scientific infallibility that few people realize they have avoided answering the criticism aimed at them. Then, having cleverly suggested that they are as scientific as their critics are romantic, the testers rest behind their statistical ramparts and calmly wait for the squall to pass.

The "statistics show..." maneuver has so powerful an effect on the layman, and even on scholars, that the test experts have come to regard it as the supreme weapon. In the battle for people's minds no general criticism can make appreciable headway against it.

If significant results are to be achieved, the critic must devise a new strategy. He must save his general criticisms till a later stage, or, at most, use them initially only in a supporting role. Instead of aiming at the central issues, he must focus on a particular weak spot in the testers' defences, find a way to turn their favorite weapons into boomerangs, and so cause the testers, in their attempts to defend themselves with improvised weapons, to expose some of their shortcomings to public view.

Not only does such a strategy exist, but it is one of extreme simplicity; the critic merely exhibits defective multiple-choice questions, declares that they are defective, and challenges the test-makers publicly to defend these, their own questions, *specifically.*

The testers intensely dislike this sort of challenge. It puts them in a quandary. They have to be wary of conceding that the questions are bad and claiming that bad questions are rare exceptions, for they do not know how many more examples the challenger has in reserve. On the other hand, if they defend a specific bad question by their "statistics show..." maneuver, they risk the implication that their use of statistics is improper **or that their statistics are untrustworthy; for if a question is manifestly bad, statistics can not properly prove it to be good.**[34]

---

34 Banesh Hoffmann, *The Tyranny of Testing,* pp. 155–156, boldface emphasis added, italicized emphasis in the original.

It is worth pausing here to consider what Hoffmann is actually saying, and what he has been doing in his own critique of the philosophy of the standardized test, for he has, indeed, concentrated on *actual specific test questions*. What Hoffmann has in effect done is to publish the "playbook" of the test-maker, and to suggest a strategy and tactics by which to confront *any* standardized test—including Common Core—and its defenders.

First, look at the basic operational strategy of the test-defender as he outlines its salient *steps:*

1) The defender *feigns patience and empathy* with the test-critic, he "makes a show of patient reasonableness" as Hoffmann puts it;
2) The defender then resorts to a subtle form of *argument from authority*, by stressing the professional competence and expertise of the test-question compilers (and recall Farley's account of how he, a non-expert, was hired to write questions for tests!); and finally,
3) The defender buttresses all of these postures with what Hoffmann calls their "statistics show..." maneuver.

Now note the strategies and tactics that Hoffmann has been employing all along to expose the specious claims of the testers:

1) He has sought, and received, from the test-takers themselves, actual samples of test questions which demonstrated ambiguity, or worse, a blatant *lack* of expertise on the part of the "experts," as was the case with the National Merit Scholarship candidate. The tactic is simple, and especially applicable to Common Core: *seek out, and demand, specific examples of questions, gathering examples of ambiguous or questions exposing the* **incompetence** *of the testers; additionally, it becomes imperative to insist on disclosure of the actual test-makers' identities, for "expertise" in any subject cannot be asserted on the basis of anonymity or protecting "professional" or "proprietary" secrets.* If such a claim *is* successfully asserted, it becomes an argument *against* the "scientific" and "objective" nature of such tests, and collapses into an argument of faith and authority to be accepted on the basis of the mere *assertion* of claims to "objectivity."
2) Once a sufficient basis is established, the way is then open to invalidate the statistics, and thereby the claim that such tests are objective and scientific, *for if statistics have been compiled on the basis of a consistent display of dubiously constructed questions persistent as a phenomenon over time, the*

claim for such tests is invalidated. At best the only claim that remains for them to make is that they have been part of the cause of spreading and rewarding mediocrity in intellectual achievement.

When formulated in this fashion, the possible reasons for secrecy in the testing business and educational establishment, as well as in the rich and powerful individuals and foundations *backing* them, become more apparent, for it becomes possible to conceive that it is *their* **own** lack of intellectual brilliance, their own mediocrity and inability to think creatively, that they seek to conceal.[35]

3. The Strategies and Tactics of Defense of Standardized Tests in Practice: The Science Questions and Hoffmann's Battle with the Education Testing Service

Hoffmann supplies an example both of the testers' defensive tactics and strategies, and his own offensive ones, by reviewing a particularly egregious case of the lack of expertise of the "experts" taken from a real question on science contained in one of their "objective, scientific" tests. As this is one of the most important examples in his book, we will spend some time reviewing it, and it appears, significantly enough, in the sixteenth chapter of his book, a chapter titled "Einstein Slighted."

The example seems innocent and straightforward enough:

> Here is question 54 in *Science*. It is listed as belonging to chemistry and its degree of difficulty is said to be "average."
> "54. The burning of gasoline in an automobile cylinder involves all of the following *except*
>   (A) reduction
>   (B) decomposition
>   (C) an exothermic reaction
>   (D) oxidation
>   (E) conversion of matter into energy"

---

35 As we shall see in the next and future chapters, this possibility becomes more and more apparent as one delves into the aims and objectives of the rise of standardized tests and the wealthy and powerful people backing them.

The average chemistry student quickly picks the wanted answer E, doubtless arguing that conversion of matter into energy refers to nuclear reactions and is thus inappropriate here.[36]

But as we have come to expect by now, the "experts" are anything but, and Hoffmann, a member of Princeton's Institute for Advanced Study, and a personal friend of Albert Einstein, was not about to let this gaffe go unpunished, statistics or no statistics.

As always, Hoffmann's critique zeroes in on the student who is more than average, and well-informed about the implications of recent advances in physics:

> But the student who is unfortunate enough to understand, even if only in an elementary way, what $E=mc^2$ is really about finds himself at a distinct disadvantage. He knows that in certain nuclear reactions energy is released through the breaking of nuclear bonds. He knows too that in the burning of gasoline the energy released comes from the dissociation of chemical bonds, that these chemical bonds contribute, however minutely, to the rest mass of the substances involved in the reaction, and that the released energy—all of it—comes from the diminution of this rest mass. Thus here, just as in our nuclear reactions, there is "conversion of matter into energy." So the superior student correctly concludes that none of the given answers is correct.
>
> One might try to defend the question by saying that since matter is a form of energy, answer E is tautological. But, quite apart from the fact that the wording is customary, any tautology would make E *a fortiori* valid, and thus unacceptable as an answer.[37]

While this might seem at first glance to be Hoffmann's typical critique, it is not, for as he goes on to observe, this critique first appeared in an article of his in *Harper's Magazine*, critiquing standardized tests.[38]

Such was the strength of this critique that the testing corporation responsible for compiling the test, the Educational Testing Service in Princeton, New Jersey, was compelled to defend the question in a pamphlet; and here is where the fun began (at least, for Hoffmann):

---

36 Banesh Hoffmann, *The Tyranny of Testing*, p. 185.

37 Ibid., pp. 185–186.

38 Ibid., p. 186.

Explanation—The superior student is as aware of the *classical* concepts of matter and chemical change as he is of the model of *modern* physics. He is likely to be more aware than is the average student that the "conversion of matter into energy" has been demonstrated only for nuclear changes. Perhaps he realizes that if the energy freed by the burning of gasoline comes from the conversion of mass to energy, the loss in mass is only about a ten-billionth of the mass of the gasoline burned, a loss too small to be measured by available methods.

When such a student is faced with the above question, he should realize that the classical concepts of matter and chemical change provide the framework in which the question is asked. He also recognizes that the first four processes listed are obviously and immediately involved in the burning of gasoline, and he selects response E as the required answer.[39]

Doubtless, the ETS thought that Hoffmann, like most other critics, would accept this seemingly plausible explanation, and allow the gaffe—and the statistics based upon it—to pass.

Not so.

In fact, as Hoffmann points out, the ETS "defense" only dug their "experts" into a position that was untenable and indefensible:

Note, for example, the curious implication of the words I emphasize in this passage: "... the 'conversion of matter into energy' has been demonstrated ONLY for nuclear changes. Perhaps he realizes that IF the energy freed by the burning of gasoline comes from the conversion of mass to energy...." Are they not intended to suggest that there is reasonable doubt that $E=mc^2$ applies to chemical as well as to nuclear processes? Does one not receive the impression that, in order to defend its question, ETS is prepared, if necessary, to abandon $E=mc^2$?[40]

Lest this critique seem obscure, or a *reductio ad absurdum* that is itself absurd, Hoffmann unpacks it in a lengthy and telling passage, exposing the ETS' "experts" and the ambiguous nature of the question itself. Ponder the following passage carefully:

---

39 Banesh Hoffmann, *The Tyranny of Testing*, p. 186. Hoffmann gives no publication data concerning the ETS pamphlet in which this passage occurs.

40 Ibid., p. 187.

Again, the remark that the loss of mass is "too small to be measured by available methods" may well impress the non-specialist, yet it is incorrect as stated. **The mass can be measured by measuring the amount of energy released and using Einstein's formula, E=mc².** Even if it were true, the remark would hardly be relevant to the crucial question here of whether mass is or is not converted into energy in the burning of gasoline. **Can ETS produce a competent physicist or chemist who would risk his reputation by denying in public that, according to current concepts, ALL of the released energy comes from the conversion of rest mass? If ALL the released energy comes from this conversion, the process is certainly not a negligible one here, though ETS would have us think otherwise.**[41]

Having dispatched of this "defense," Hoffmann then engages with the implicit assumption ETS is making regarding what it is calling "classical" concepts, and once again, demolishes the assumptions of mind-reading ability that ETS—in its scientific and objective wisdom—is asking the test-taker to perform on this question:

Having tried to undermine E=mc², ETS next tries a different tack. Implicitly admitting the validity of E=mc², it says that the superior student "should realize that the classical concepts of matter and chemical change provide the framework in which the question is asked." **Einstein's formula, E=mc², is over fifty years old. Why should the superior student realize that he is to use only those concepts that ETS chooses to regard as "classical"?**[42]

As if this is not enough, Hoffmann exposes the *duplicitous* nature of the question:

We now come to a crucial question: **why was the non-"classical," relativistic answer included among the choices?**

Why indeed, if the test-taker was to think solely in "classical" terms? Was the inclusion of the relativistic answer designed to highlight this fact? Or was it to obfuscate the question so hopelessly that no answer could reasonably be chosen? Hoffmann homes in:

---

41 Banesh Hoffmann, *The Tyranny of Testing*, p. 187, emphasis added.
42 Ibid., emphasis added.

Was this answer put there deliberately, or was the ETS at the time it framed the question unaware of the meaning of E=mc^2?

Note how damaging are the implications if we assume, as perhaps ETS wishes us to, that ETS was fully aware of the meaning of E=mc^2 and deliberately included answer E nevertheless. For we must then ask: what was its motive for doing so? To make a question with no correct answer? Let us hope not. Then what? To penalize the superior student? One doubts that ETS would say so; yet the question is surely easier for the student who does not understand E=mc^2 than for the student who does. Is the latter student supposed *to compensate for the deficiencies of the test-maker by reading possibly hazardous amendments into the question as worded—into a science question, moreover?*[43]

Indeed, from the wording of ETS' initial "defense" of the question in response to Mr. Hoffmann's *Harper's Magazine* article, it would seem that ETS *did* want to penalize the superior student, for its entire "defense" is predicated on the "superior" student being able to read the minds of the anonymous test-makers and to opt for its own definitions of "classical" physics concepts.

The *other* alternative, a malicious intention to obfuscate and be duplicitous, is too awful to contemplate. Nonetheless, Hoffmann, in guarded language that concludes his "Einstein Slighted" chapter, implies that this may have been the case; answering the question with which he ended in the above quotation, he continues:

> That way lies chaos, not "objectivity." If the superior student does decide to pick answer E, does he not do so with contempt for the test-maker, and with cynical disregard of scientific facts? Should he be rewarded for his willingness to place expediency above scientific integrity? If tests are training students to respond in this way, are they not having a deleterious effect on education?
>
> Perhaps, after all, it is more charitable to assume that ETS was ignorant of the meaning of E=mc^2 when it framed the question, even if this does imply a certain lack of candor on its part now.[44]

This was not, however, the only problem on a science question that Hoffmann used to illustrate the strategies and tactics of defense, or, in this case, *avoidance of the admission of a huge blunder,* on the part of the test-makers.

---

43 Banesh Hoffmann, *The Tyranny of Testing*, pp. 187–188, all emphases added.
44 Banesh Hoffmann, *The Tyranny of Testing*, p. 188.

The authors advise the careful reader who is interested in a further example with more detailed commentary by Dr. Hoffmann to read the appendix at the end of this chapter. For the sake of brevity and for having already provided evidence of Dr. Hoffmann's excellent analysis, we must now ask the reader to consider why we, with Dr. Hoffmann, raise intellectual arms in such a duel with the Testing Services?

Here, we would respectfully disagree with the late Dr. Hoffmann, for it is not so much piquant, but pathetic and reprehensible.

In his duel with the Educational Testing Service and its very inept "defenses" of flawed question after question, Dr. Hoffmann reveals a deeper psychopathy, narcissism, and sense of entitlement in the "educational elite," for the Educational Testing Service "and other test-makers are ready to plead for just enough special laxity in the interpretation of words to *allow them* to escape from an awkward position even though they *deny the candidate* equivalent latitude on the ground that the test is objective."[45]

Like all elites of mediocrity, the edugarchy cannot suffer its own incompetence to be exposed, and hence, must resort to the time-honored traditions of entitlement and double standard. While many more examples—both contemporary and older—might be included here, we believe that with the testimony of Farley, a "testing insider" and that of Dr. Hoffmann, sufficient examples have been provided for the reader to begin to question the whole philosophy of any program of standardized testing, including, and *especially*, the adaptive assessment process of Common Core, for here one is confronted not only with an "experts soviet" determining anonymously and unaccountably what answers are "correct," and an equally empowered and anonymous elite of "experts" programing the computers *assessing* such tests, one now adds a *third* layer of experts in "child psychology" and "education" that will determine personality types, individual responses, and the individually adapted questions and "acceptable answers" to them.

Indeed, as Dr. Hoffmann pointed out when his articles and book first appeared in the 1950s and 1960s, the U.S. Air Force conducted such tests beginning in 1943 during the height of the Second World War, and continued them into the mid-1950s. The results were compiled and examined by Professors Robert L. Thorndike and Elizabeth Hagen of Columbia University's Teachers College, in a book published in 1959 titled *Ten Thousand Careers*.[46]

---

45 Ibid., p. 183, emphasis added.
46 Banesh Hoffmann, The Tyranny of Testing, pp. 146–147.

Citing what he calls their "carefully worded verdict,"[47] they and Hoffmann raise a significant question:

> As far as we were able to determine from our data, there is no convincing evidence that aptitude tests or biographical information of the type that was available to us can predict degree of success within an occupation insofar as this is represented in the criterion measures that we were able to obtain. This would suggest that we should view the long-range prediction of occupational success by aptitude tests with a good deal of skepticism and take a very restrained view as to how much can be accomplished in this direction.[48]

But if this be the case, then why the postwar push for not only continued but expanded use of such tests, a push that has continued to our own time and manifest itself with the latest educational panacea and snake oil, Common Core?

With this question, we return to "Robert/a," the vapid twit, the facilitator-as-commissar, whom Farley encountered, and whom we encountered at the beginning of this chapter. In such a world, where one is tested relentlessly from grade school to corporate "meetings" or, for professional teachers, in mind-numbing "continuing education" seminars in which they are forced to drink the laudanum-laced snake oil of "experts and facilitators," what is the common purpose? Why is there such widespread punishment of individual creativity and brilliance, the punishment of the "finer mind" as Jacques Barzun put it in his Foreword to Hoffmann's book? Why did we encounter occasions where there may have even been evident duplicity in the "forceful use" of wrong answers? Where does the mediocrity and implicit deception evident in the standardized test come from? *Why is it there?* And why are so many subjected to ongoing versions of those tests in the form of the facilitator-led meeting, meetings which, like the standardized tests, are studies in passive aggression, submission to consensus and conformity, and which in the final analysis, are revealed as nothing but loyalty and conformity exercises?

Is the whole effort really not about education, but about something else?

To answer that question, we must look at the succession—personal, institutional, and conceptual—of the education episcopacy.

---

47 Ibid., p. 148.
48 Cited in Hoffmann, *The Tyranny of Testing*, p. 148.

4. An Appendix

We freely admit, when we read this next exchange between Hoffmann and the ETS, we *had* to laugh out loud, and we seriously considered writing the Educational Testing Service and suggesting that it change its name to the Educational Twittery Service. Consider, Hoffmann proposes, the following physics question that appeared on a test, and about which Hoffmann again wrote an article for *Harper's Magazine*, again trying to warn Americans about what was happening in their "education" system as a result of standardized tests:

65. Potassium metal loses electrons when struck by light (the photoelectric effect) more readily than lithium metal because
    (A) the potassium atom contains more protons than does that of lithium
    (B) the valence electron of potassium is farther from the nucleus than is that of lithium
    (C) potassium occurs above lithium in the electro-chemical series
    (D) the potassium atom contains more electrons than does that of lithium
    (E) the potassium nuclear is larger than that of lithium.[49]

Hoffmann observes that the answer wanted as the correct answer for this question was answer B, but, he asks, was it the *best* answer?[50]

And thus began the next round between Hoffmann and the Educational Testing Service, for he noted that there are at least three other possible answers offered that "are not only factual statements in themselves but could be defended as more satisfactory answers than B."[51] Thus, one begins by assuming that there is a more well-informed student answering this question. He or she immediately sees that answer B is possible, for the valence electron of potassium is indeed farther away from the potassium nucleus than is lithium's valence electron.

But he then sees that answer D accurately (if ungrammatically) states the reason *why* this is so, namely that "the potassium atom contains more electrons than does that of lithium." Thus, the student may sensibly conclude that while B is

49 Ibid., p. 189. For the reference to its appearance as an example in his Harper's Magazine article, see p. 191.
50 Ibid.
51 Banesh Hoffmann, *The Tyranny of Testing*, pp. 189–190.

a correct answer, D is a correct answer too. And D **is a more profound answer than B.**

But our student is not finished. For he realizes that the reason why there are more electrons in the potassium atom than in the lithium atom is to be found in answer A: the atom of potassium "contains more protons than does that of lithium." Thus, if D is a correct answer, so is A. And A cuts deeper than D.

Finally, he hesitates to dismiss E, knowing that the nucleus of potassium "is larger than that of lithium" because it contains more neutrons and protons. Thus, if A is a correct answer, so also is E.

In view of the above, most of us would agree with the College Board that the question is "difficult." But with us this is merely a matter of opinion. With the test experts it is an objective, scientific, no-nonsense fact based on statistics. **Of course, the statistics do not reveal that the wording of the question is vague. Nor that, if the wanted answer is a correct one, so are three others. Nor that the examiners have chosen the most immediate and superficial answer, thus penalizing candidates with more probing minds, as they so often do.** Can we be complacent when we know that such questions are used by so many of our colleges to assess scientific talent?[52]

By pointing out the ambiguity and superficiality of the question and its "correct" answer, Hoffmann is once again throwing light on the value and validity of the appeal to statistics, for if statistics are compiled on the basis of faulty questions, what is their value for the claim that such tests are scientific and objective, and measure anything but the incompetence of the test-makers?

Needless to say, the ETS had to respond Hoffmann's critique, and Hoffman notes that it made "a long defense of this question." Indeed, Hoffmann observes,

Though it is not addressed solely to the specialist, it is inevitably rather technical. Read it through nevertheless. It is written with such an air of reasoned confidence and scientific logic that the non-specialist will feel convinced that it is a devastating rebuttal of an utterly base and utterly baseless criticism. Yet in fact, as will be demonstrated, it is so gravely damaging to ETS that that organization would far better have kept silent and allowed the challenge to stand against it unanswered.[53]

---

52 Ibid., p. 190, emphasis added.
53 Banesh Hoffmann, *The Tyranny of Testing*, p. 191.

With that, Hoffmann reproduces the Educational Testing Service's easy, breezy, "ironclad scientific" defense of the question.

Explanation — The technical terms must be considered in studying this question. The photoelectric effect is exhibited by an element if, in atoms of the element, an electron is so loosely bound that visible light provides enough energy to free that electron from its atom. Since electrons are negatively charged, most of them are too strongly attracted to the positively charged atomic nucleus to be freed by light. The farther from the nucleus an electron is found, the more likely it is that light will be able to free the electron and that the photoelectric effect will be observed.

Since the outer—or valence—electron of a potassium atom, on the average, is farther from the nucleus than the valence electron of a lithium atom, of these two the element that shows the photoelectric effect is potassium. Response B, the accepted response to this question, is based on this reasoning.

Dr. Hoffmann agrees to accept B and then begins to study other responses to see whether they can account for B. He reasons that if B is the cause of the photoelectric effect and if D is the cause of B, then D must be the cause of this effect.

Cause-effect relations in science are difficult to reduce to the confines of one response to a multiple-choice question; to find a chain of causes, such as Dr. Hoffmann proposes, in a single question would be most surprising, but we must look.

It is quite true that if one limits his consideration to a family of elements, like the one that contains potassium and lithium, the greater the number of electrons in an atom, the farther from the nucleus is the outer electron likely to be found. Is there a cause-effect relation here? Potassium has 19 electrons, calcium has 20; yet the outer electron of the calcium atom, on the average, is closer to the nucleus than is the valence electron of potassium. Indeed, of the elements whose atoms have progressively more electrons than potassium, krypton, with 36 electrons, is the first element for whose atoms the outer electron is normally farther from the nucleus than is the valence electron of a potassium atom. A larger number of electrons in an atom clearly does not "cause" the outer electron of an atom to be farther from its atomic nucleus. If D does not "cause" B, it can hardly be said to "cause" the photoelectric effect. The other responses cited by Dr. Hoffmann as "causes" of the effect can be criticized in the same fashion.[54]

---

54 Banesh Hoffmann, *The Tyranny of Testing*, pp. 191–192. Emphasis added.

This all sounds perfectly plausible, reasonable, and scientific.

But Hoffmann wasn't buying, and when we first read this "defense," neither were we. Hoffmann, as usual, minces no words, and again, due to their importance, we cite his response at length.

> This is a remarkable defence, well worth examination in detail because **of what it reveals of both the caliber and the tactics of ETS.**
>
> When ETS says that "the photoelectric effect is exhibited... if... an electron is so loosely bound that *visible* light provides enough energy to free that electron...," and, later, that "... of these to [potassium and lithium] the element that shows the photoelectric effect is potassium," there is no escaping the conclusion that it believes not only that the photoelectric effect is confined to visible light, but also that the effect is not exhibited by lithium.
>
> **These are incredibly elementary blunders.** And, apparently because of them, ETS does not even understand what its own question is about. It clearly believes here that its question asks for the cause of the photoelectric effect. The evidence is conclusive. Note the context of this sentence at the end of the second paragraph of its defence: "Response b, the accepted response... is based on this reasoning." Note, too, the words: "He reasons that if B is *the cause of the photoelectric effect* and if D is the cause of B then D must be *the cause of this effect*," "If D does not 'cause' B, it can hardly be said to '*cause' the photoelectric effect*," and "The other responses cited by Dr. Hoffmann as '*causes' of the effect*..."
>
> Now, of course, I did not cite responses as causes of the photoelectric effect as ETS asserts. I addressed myself to the actual question, not to what ETS imagined the question to be. Both potassium and lithium exhibit the photoelectric effect, as any competent chemist or physicist knows, and the question asks why "potassium metal loses electrons MORE READILY than lithium metal." Does ETS expect the superior student to read possibly hazardous amendments into this question too? **How can the superior student hope to guess what is in the examiner's mind when the examiner makes so many unpredictable blunders?**[55]

Why are these "unpredictable blunders"?

---

55 Banesh Hoffmann, The Tyranny of Testing, pp. 192–193, italicized and capitalized emphases Hoffmann's, boldface emphases added.

Because, as Hoffmann points out, the Educational Testing Service's "correct answer," answer B, does *not* "give the cause of the photoelectric effect" either, and the reason is very simple and well-known: "The crucial quantity" involved in the photoelectric effect, he reminds the "experts" at ETS, "is not distance from the nucleus but the amount of energy needed to remove the electron from the metal, and this depends in a quite complicated way on the state of the metal."[56] In other words, the effect depends on a *constellation* of factors, lattice structure, and therefore, the number of protons, electrons, distance, the position of the valence shell, and ultimately the amount of energy required to create the effect under variable conditions of each metal. But it most decidedly is *not* merely matter of "distance" as the Educational Testing Service initially framed its "defense," and the other answers that Hoffmann explored are illustrative of these other factors in any student's mind who knew the effect with any degree of competence!

Hoffmann, however, was not done. "Let us now look," he states, "at the maneuver by which ETS seeks to convince the reader that though answer B is acceptable, answers D, A, and E are not."[57] The maneuver is simple obfuscation and concealment, an obfuscation and concealment that only a real expert would uncover, but one that, nonetheless, exposes ETS' defense for what it was: a sophisticated form of deception, *or* an egregious case of incompetence, and in either case, an example of fraud:

> The maneuver is a simple one: by speaking loosely of "the valence electron" and "the outer electron," ETS enlarges the scope of the question by suggesting that it applies to several elements, and not just to lithium and potassium. Using this enlargement of scope, ETS denies that answer B is a consequence of answer D; that is, ETS denies that the fact that the valence electron of potassium is farther from the nucleus is a consequence of the fact that the potassium atom contains more electrons. It cites the fact that though the calcium atom has more electrons than potassium its "outer" electron is essentially closer to its nucleus. And it triumphantly points out that "of the elements whose atoms have progressively more electrons than potassium [which has only 19], krypton, with 36 electrons, is the first element of whose atoms the 'outer' electron is normally farther from the nucleus than is the valence electron of potassium."
>
> This seems like a superb triumph. But the triumph proves illusory, for the argument boomerangs. If ETS wishes to claim that answer B is valid

---

56 Ibid., p. 193.
57 Banesh Hoffmann, The Tyranny of Testing, p. 194.

when the scope of the question is enlarged it must, from the wording of answer B, believe that the farther an electron is from the nucleus the more readily it escapes from the atom when struck by light. But, as ETS itself points out, the "outer" electron of krypton is normally farther away from the nucleus than is the valence electron of potassium. This being so, **how does ETS propose to account for the awkward fact that krypton does *not* lose electrons when struck by light more readily than the potassium atom does?**

ETS can not have it both ways. To make answer B acceptable it must limit the number of elements involved, in which case it can not legitimately deny that answer D causes answer B, and that A causes D. In denying that D causes B it allows many types of elements to enter, but in that case its triumphant argument against answer D destroys its own case for answer B and shows that no answer is valid.[58]

So what, *really*, is the point of all this? Hoffmann, like Farley, reduces it to its simplest form, for these "defenses" were all offered in a pamphlet issued by the Educational Testing Service called *Explanation of Multiple-Choice Testing*, in the preface to which it defended its answers, even in questions Hoffman—who is mentioned by name—criticized, by noting that there were "detailed reasons which convinced panels of judges that they were good questions."[59]

Precisely.

It is about *conformity* to an anonymous soviet of experts and their consensus, and hence, about *consensus* reality rather than about *reasoning ability* and *facts*. Hoffmann observes that when the preface is read as "postscript rather than preamble" that the admission that the "correct answers" convinced "panels of judges" takes on "a piquant quality."[60]

---

58 Banesh Hoffmann, The Tyranny of Testing, pp. 194–195, bold emphasis added.
59 Ibid., p. 195.
60 Ibid.

Elites, Educators, Facilitators, and Foundations

Part One: Wundt, Americans, and
Teachers as Change Agents

"I have been guilty of my share of educational banalities."

—

JAMES BRYANT CONANT[1]

"Standardized exams were developed as markers of failure, and stood as justifications for and symbols of the changes the reformers sought."

—

MARK J. GARRISON[2]

C onsider the following statements, which are deliberately presented—for the moment—with no context, that is to say, with
no indication of who composed these words, nor when, nor for
what purpose:

Within a few years the number of adolescents in this country will be 50 per
cent greater than at present. Looking forward to that time, I suggest that:

(1) We do not expand our four-year colleges either as to number or as
to size.

(2) We do not expand our four-year programs in our universities; rather,
we contract them.

---

1   James Bryant Conant, Ph.D., *The Revolutionary Transformation of the American
    High School* (Cambridge, MA: Harvard University Press, 1959), p. 1.
2   Mark J. Garrison, *A Measure of Failure: The Political Origins of Standardized Testing*
    (Albany, NY: SUNY Press, 2009), p. 3.

(3) We attempt to make a two-year college course (following the regular high school course) fashionable; to this end we might award a bachelor's degree of general studies to the graduates of such colleges.

(4) We endeavor to create a climate of opinion in which the length of education beyond eighteen is *not* considered the hallmark of its respectability.

(5) We continue the expansion of our junior and senior high schools to meet the new bulge in enrollments, but in so doing, **recognize the need for remaking the curriculum in many schools.**

(6) We adhere to the principle of a comprehensive high school **with a common core of studies and differentiated special programs,** but in so doing we **make far more effort to identify the gifted youth and give him or her more rigorous training in languages and mathematics.** ...

Our (for the moment) anonymous commentator continues in this fashion through four more paragraphs, to make four more enumerated points.

The reader will have noted one significant and obvious clue, however, as to *when* this series of recommendations might have been composed, for the reference to the creation of a two-year college degree—the "associate's degree" now presented in many local community and junior colleges—was presented as a future goal, and since the associate's degree only began to become truly widespread in the 1980s, one may assume the above recommendations preceded this period.

More importantly, however, the reader may have noticed some disturbing implications of points five and six, for on the one hand our anonymous commentator argues that the swelling numbers into American junior and senior high schools calls for a "remaking of the curriculum," while on the other hand he (or she) calls for a "common core of studies and differentiated special programs" in addition to an intensified effort to "identify gifted youth and give him or her more rigorous training in languages and mathematics." This implies that the "remade curriculum" and "common core of studies" being advocated in point five and at the beginning of point six are really a curriculum that has been deliberately designed to serve the lowest common educational ability, thus making the special provisions to identify gifted students and give them "more rigorous training in languages and mathematics" necessary.

Consequently, the program being advocated is nothing less than a massive expansion of the availability of education at the middle-school through the first two years of college level, while at the same time a dumbing-down of the curriculum at these levels, with a special "sorting mechanism" being put into place to identify and "more rigorously educate" the gifted students. And the subtle implication here is that the anonymous commentator making all these recommendations is himself (or herself) a member of an elite.

In short, the plan being suggested is nothing less than the organization of a "caste system," with education itself as the mechanism driving it. The purpose of this "caste" system will become clearer as we proceed.

The individual making these recommendations was James Bryant Conant, Ph.D. (1893–1978), the President of Harvard University from 1933 to 1953 (whose gecko-like visage appears below), in a book which appeared during his last year of tenure at the helm of Harvard, *Education and Liberty: The Role of Schools in a Modern Democracy.*[3] That Conant's recommendations, particularly with respect to the formation of the two-year college associate's degree, came to pass some decades later is a testimony to the power and influence this individual had within the formation of the modern (and broken) American educational system.

JAMES BRYANT CONANT, PH.D. 1893–1978,
HARVARD UNIVERSITY PRESIDENT, 1933–1953

---

3   James Bryant Conant, *Education and Liberty: The Role of Schools in a Modern Democracy* (Cambridge, MA: Harvard University Press, 1953), p. 57, italicized emphasis in the original, boldface emphasis added.

A. Common Core Standards and the Common Core Assessment Process: Two Different Things, and a Clever Strategy

The reader will have noted that our focus thus far has been on the widespread use of the standardized test within American education. The reason for this is that while the Common Core standards look and sound good on paper, in our opinion not nearly enough attention is being paid to the *assessment process* for the standards. Indeed, in our opinion, the discussion seems to be deliberately focused *away* from that process to the standards themselves, when in actual fact, the heart of Common Core is the assessment process and the questions it raises: 1) who wrote the questions? 2) what are the algorithms for assessing individual responses to the computerized tests that are at the heart of Common Core?

And so on.

When the Common Core standards are viewed from the standpoint of the assessment process, it becomes clear that the result will be the further entrenchment of what some have called "the Great American Education-Industrial Complex,"[4] and that the end result will be the dumbing-down process we have witnessed during the last century, on steroids. Or to put it in a slightly different way, each new "fad" that has been promoted in American education since the rise of the progressive education movement in the late nineteenth and early twentieth century is really "about shifts in power and purpose, not 'school improvement.'"[5] As Mark J. Garrison notes, standardized tests are at the core of the issue:

> Rendering the crisis in education and society as a fabrication of the elite veils why the elite (the bankers, industrialists, and key politicians) would work so hard to destroy that which those in their position one hundred fifty years ago worked so hard to build as necessary for maintaining their political system and their power? On what basis is this institution—public education—no longer serving its functions, from their point of view? Why use tests to discredit this institution when they proved so useful in establishing it? And what significance and opening does this crisis have for defending rights and for people's genuine empowerment and public participation?[6]

---

4   Anthony G. Picciano and Joel Spring, *The Great American Education-Industrial Complex: Ideology, Technology, and Profit* (New York: Routledge, 2013).

5   Mark J. Garrison, *A Measure of Failure: The Political Origins of Standardized Testing* (Albany, NY: The State University of New York Press, 2009), p. 4.

6   Mark J. Garrison, *A Measure of Failure*, p. 4.

Garrison answers his own questions by noting that any system of educational standards imposed by any elite—political or corporate—is really an assertion of sovereignty and power, "as a means to give material expression to a philosophy or aim, and as embodiments of the social values of a culture or class."[7]

As such, standardized testing or "psychometry" really developed as a tool employed by the elite classes "for vertical classification and the production of social value,"[8] that is to say, standardized testing was really developed as a sorting mechanism to determine those the elite understood to be most suited to form a "natural aristocracy" with the "right to govern." Intellectual ability—at least as the standardized tests defined it—was linked to that right.[9] But as we have also seen, such tests in the end punish, rather than reward, real ability, *with the end result that such tests really measure the ability of an individual to conform to the outlook and interests of the elites composing such tests*:

> The question then is not so much whether standardization is "bad" or "good" but whose interests does such standardization serve, what outlook does it reflect, and so on. ... (The) aim of "testing by a standard" is not standardization of that which is tested, but uniform differentiation. This is a variant of equal treatment consistent with the democratic norm of political equality. In educational assessment, it is not the standardization of students, but rather the standardization of measurers that is at issue, a standardization that bolsters a central power, its aim, outlook, and so on.[10]

These observations therefore require a closer look at the "educational oligarchy" or "edugarchy" and at the history of its rise.

B. The Education Episcopacy, the Testing Theocracy, and the Wundtian Succession
1. Conant and the Revolutionary Transformation of the American High School

We may describe this history as a kind of "episcopal" or "apostolic succession," i.e., as a succession of *individuals* in certain positions of authority who are

---

7   Ibid.
8   Ibid., p. 5.
9   Ibid.
10 Mark J. Garrison, *A Measure of Failure*, p. 20.

in direct contact with each other, but also as a succession of the "educational faith" or core ideas passed from one to the other. Our entry into this survey will once again be Dr. James Bryant Conant, and his 1959 Inglis lecture titled, suggestively enough, "The Revolutionary Transformation of the American High School."

At the beginning of his lecture Conant asks whether the great transformation of American education from 1905 to 1930 was "comparable to prohibition, or to the change in our transportation? In short, is it or is it not a reversible social process?"[11] In other words, was the transformation the result of a deliberate policy being imposed through political power (Prohibition), or was it merely the result of a constellation of social and cultural forces, and hence not the deliberate act of people working in concert to impose it? Conant answers his question immediately: "For those who are familiar with the employment picture in the United States, to ask this question is to answer it."[12] He points out that with so many young people unemployed, and leaving family farms in rural areas, a demographic picture compounded by the Depressions of 1907 and 1929, high school education naturally expanded to encompass virtually the whole American population as unemployed youth were absorbed by the school system.[13] Having thus deflected any notions of "conspiracy," Conant does, however, offer a salient bit of carefully worded backpedaling: "Let me make it plain," he states,

> ...that in stressing the alteration in the employment scene I do not mean to imply that educators had no influence on the transformation of the high school. The true interpretation of the revolutionary transformation of secondary education lies between the two extremes I earlier depicted.[14]

Later in the lecture, he expands on this by referring to a 1918 report of the National Education Association (*Cardinal Principles of Secondary Education*)[15]

---

11 James Bryant Conant, *The Revolutionary Transformation of the American High School*, p. 9.

12 Ibid., pp. 9–10.

13 See Conant's discussion, *The Revolutionary Transformation of the American High School*, pp. 10–11. Conant conveniently ignores, of course, the action of America's major banks in precipitating both Depressions leading to this situation. We shall have occasion to observe the interlock between American finance capitalism and education during this period later in this chapter.

14 Ibid., p. 11.

15 Ibid., p. 14.

and the writings of John Dewey, and remarks that he was "struck" by the fact that the new ideas in these works "fit" the changed social and cultural conditions "as a key fits in a lock."[16] His next words are revealing:

> Confronted with a "heterogeneous high school population destined to enter all sorts of occupations," high school teachers and administrators and professors of education needed some justification **for a complete overhauling of a high school curriculum originally designed for a homogeneous student body.** The progressives with their emphasis on the child, "on learning by doing," on democracy and citizenship, **and with their attacks on the arguments used to support a classical curriculum,** were bringing up just the sort of *new* ideas that were sorely needed.[17]

Note that what Conant is really suggesting here is that at the minimum the "progressive educators" seized on a social transformation as a "crisis of opportunity" by which to impose a new curriculum, one aimed not so much at the instruction in classical subjects and critical independent thinking, but rather at the role of "democracy and citizenship," i.e., at teaching certain behaviors and social values.

> And here we meet the reforming zeal of the educator and recognize it as one, but only one, of the factors in the process which transformed the high school. The NEA Commission, arguing that secondary education was essential for *all* youth, made the following specific recommendation: "*Consequently this Commission holds that education should be so reorganized that every normal boy and girl will be encouraged to remain in school to the age of 18 on full time if possible, other wise* [sic] *on part time.*"[18]

This was, of course, a huge seizure of power on the part of the edugarchy, for it now meant that its recommendation of compulsory education through eighteen years or the twelfth grade[19] exposed young people to the philosophy of the professional educators not only in childhood but through adolescence.

---

16 Ibid., p. 15.

17 Ibid., pp. 15–16, boldface emphasis added, italicized emphasis in the original.

18 James Bryant Conant, *The Revolutionary Transformation of the American High School*, pp. 17–18, italicized emphasis in the original.

19 Ibid., pp. 19, 23, for the context of the Smith-Hughes Act of 1917, requiring compulsory education through the twelfth grade, including vocational training.

Conant also makes yet another astonishing, carefully worded statement:

> No one could attempt to assay the relative contributions made by the professional educators acting directly on the content of the high school curriculum and the other group—labor leaders, humanitarian reformers—whose ideas and actions changed the framework within which the high school teachers had to operate.[20]

Why is this astonishing?

Consider Conant's actual carefully worded argument thus far:

1) There was no "educational conspiracy" to revolutionarily transform American education;
2) The transformation was solely the result of social and economic conditions;
3) These conditions were nevertheless seized upon by various elites as a "crisis of opportunity" to effect a revolutionary transformation;
4) Thus, since the real transformation was social in nature, and not the result of any real deliberate policy, "no one" can "attempt to assay the relative contributions made by the professional educators acting directly on the content of the high school curriculum..." That is to say, he has shielded those "reformers" and their reforms: since it is impossible to evaluate their successes or influences, it is impossible to hold them accountable for their failures.

So confident was Conant in the viability of these reforms that he ended his lecture with this "prophecy" (his word, not ours):

> If the free world survives the perils that now confront it, I believe historians in the year 2059 will regard the American experiment in democracy as a great and successful adventure of the human race. Furthermore, as an essential part of this adventure—indeed, as the basic element in the twentieth century—they will praise the radical transformation of America's treatment of its children and of its youth. They will regard the American high school, as it was perfected by the end of the twentieth century, as not only one of the finest products of democracy, but as a continuing insurance for the preservation of the vitality of a society of free men.[21]

---

20 Ibid., p. 12.

21 James Bryant Conant, *The Revolutionary Transformation of the American High School*, p. 29.

We stand at the approximate halfway point on the way toward Conant's prophetic prediction, and few would agree that American education is performing successfully. Notwithstanding Conant's carefully worded deflections of the real question, it nevertheless remains: is the mediocrity of American public education an accident, or was it deliberately designed to be this way? Was it deliberately designed to dumb down the general population, and to render it passive and compliant to general collectivization and Balkanization?

The answer requires a brief look at the educational reformers of the late nineteenth and early twentieth century themselves, the very reformers that Conant seeks to shield from any criticism or examination. The answer requires us to look at

2. "The Leipzig Connection": The Stimulus-Response Cosmology and the Redefinition of Education and the Teacher

In 1980, Paolo Lionni published a thin little paperback that has since become something of an underground "cult critique" of the basis of modern American education, titled *The Leipzig Connection*. The little book, now in its fifth printing, was reviewed by various newspapers around the country, some of which appear on the current printing's back cover. There, for example, one may read *The Christian Science Monitor*'s review: "Arresting... paints a picture of deliberate sabotaging of sound pedagogy... by those who should have known better." Even *The Seattle Times* weighed in with the observation "Perceptive... a blunt, concise argument for the restoration of educational principles... will stimulate argument."[22] Lionni's argument is that the American education system was not only *expanded* during the period, but that it was deliberately designed to fail as an instrument to hand down the Western cultural and scientific tradition, but that it was wildly successful at what it was really resigned to do, i.e., to produce a collectivized dumbed-down population where individuals' creative and critical thought processes were atrophied.

Lionni is not alone in this assessment. David Albert, in his Introduction to John Taylor Gatto's *Dumbing Us Down: The Hidden Curriculum of Compulsory Schooling*, pulls no punches:

---

22 Paolo Lionni, *The Leipzig Connection* (Sheridan, OR: Heron Books, 2013), back cover.

Central to this understanding is the fact that *schools are not failing*. On the contrary, they are spectacularly successful in doing what they are intended to do, and what they have been intended to do since their inception. The system, perfected at places like the University of Chicago, Columbia Teachers College, Carnegie-Mellon, and Harvard, and funded by the captains of industry, was explicitly set up to ensure a docile, malleable workforce to meet the growing, changing demands of corporate capitalism—"to meet the new demands of the 20ᵗʰ century," they would have said back then. The Combine... ensures a workforce that will not rebel—the greatest fear at the turn of the 20ᵗʰ century—that will be physically, intellectually, and emotionally dependent upon corporate institutions for their incomes, self-esteem, and stimulation, and that will learn to find social meaning in their lives solely in the production and consumption of material goods. We all grew up in these institutions and we know how they work. They haven't changed much since the 1890s because they don't need to—they perform precisely as intended.[23]

Lionni begins *his* little book by pointing out the same social transformation observed by Conant and by Albert (who obviously drew different conclusions from it than Conant!):

In the final years of the 19ᵗʰ century, a great transformation began in American education. By the end of the first world war [sic], Americans would notice increasingly a change in the way their children were being educated. In the succeeding decades, the same schools would become infested with drugs and crime, and high schools would be graduating students who could barely read, spell, or do simple arithmetic.[24]

Like Albert, Lionni fingers the "change agents" in the "edugarchy" as being the great "philanthropic" family foundations—the Ford, Carnegie, and Rockefeller Foundations—and a host of individuals in the field of "psychology."[25]

The central force in the education revolution and its widespread diffusion throughout American education was the German psychologist Wilhelm

23　David Albert, "Introduction" in John Taylor Gatto, *Dumbing Us Down: The Hidden Curriculum of Compulsory Schooling* (Gabriola Island, British Columbia: New Society Publishers, 2005), p. xx.

24　Paolo Lionni, *The Leipzig Connection*, p. ix.

25　Ibid., p. ix et passim.

Wundt.[26] Wundt initiated the "materialist turn" in psychology, in effect founding the school that would ultimately become Behaviorism,[27] for he believed if one assembled enough data "concerning physiological responses" to various stimuli, then "perceptions and experiences could be understood through measureable physiological reactions…".[28] Thus, the individual's use of human will was merely "the direct result of the combination of perceived stimuli, not an independent, individual intention as psychology and philosophy had, with some notable exceptions, held up to that time."[29] Thus, Wundt was responding to the increasingly "materialistic" cosmology of the nineteenth century, with its corresponding increase in the "mathematization" of the sciences. If psychology was to be truly "scientific," then for Wundt this implied its measurability and mathematization, and this required the reduction of man and the human psyche and its reasoning functions to purely materialistic foundations.

This implied that the individual human person was merely the sum "of his experiences, of the stimuli which intrude upon his consciousness and unconsciousness."[30] From this premise, a number of educational corollaries immediately followed.

The first corollary was that "The child… is a stimulus-response **mechanism.**"[31] As a result, the way was paved for schools to be revolutionarily transformed "more toward the socialization of the child than toward the development of intellect; and for the emergence of a society more and more blatantly devoted to the gratification of sensory desires at the expense of

---

26 Paolo Lionni, *The Leipzig Connection*, p. 4. Lionni in fact states that Wundt's "psychologization" of education had worldwide influence, though his book is focused on American education and his influence therein.

27 Ibid., p. 9, Lionni observes that Wundt's thesis lays "the philosophical basis for the principles of conditioning later developed by Pavlov," who incidentally studied psychology at—you guessed it—Wundt's University of Leipzig, where Wundt founded the first psychology laboratory all based on the principle of studying stimulus-response.

28 Ibid., p. 4.

29 Ibid., p. 5.

30 Ibid., p. 7. For the theologically inclined, this means that the person (υποστασις) is defined by its natural operations (φυσικαι ενεργειαι), wherein even the latter category is reduced to merely a material "stimulus-response" matrix. In quasi-Thomistic terms, where persona est relatio, the relationship which thus defines the person is the stimulus-response matrix.

31 Ibid., p. 9.

responsibility and achievement."[32] Consequently, a redefinition of education itself was inevitably implied:

> From Wundt's work, it was only a short step to the later redefinition of the meaning of education. Originally, education meant the drawing out of a person's innate talents and abilities by imparting the knowledge of languages, scientific reasoning, history, literature, rhetoric, etc.—the channels through which those abilities would flourish and serve. To the experimental psychologist, however, *education became the process of exposing the student to "meaningful" experiences to ensure desired reactions..."*[33]

And with this, of course, we have arrived at the dreaded personage of "the workshop facilitator," whose credentials consist precisely in the design of "meaningful" experiences, i.e., stimulus-response activities designed to reinforce certain types of behavior and perceptions of the self for those participating in them. We shall have much more to say about the "facilitator" and the crucial role in this stimulus-response and dumbing-down process later on.

C. Dewey, Counts, and the Rockefellers
1. The First Wundtian Succession: Wundt, Hall, and Dewey

Wundt's influence spread outward from his laboratory and psychology faculty at the University of Leipzig, particularly to America, during a time when so many American academics went to Germany to obtain their postgraduate degrees, in everything from medicine to physics, and, of course, psychology. Though it is an obvious fact, one should nevertheless take note of the problem that this imposes and the philosophical questions it raises, for why would American educators, products supposedly of a democratic federal republic, draw inspiration at the educational fountains of the Prussian, Imperial, Wilhelmine German *Kaiserreich*?

Part of the answer is afforded by looking at the Wundtian lines of succession in the education episcopacy. Wundt's first American student, G. Stanley Hall, joined the faculty of Johns Hopkins University in Baltimore in

---

32 Paolo Lionni, *The Leipzig Connection*, p. 9.
33 Ibid., p. 8.

1883.[34] Hall founded the psychology laboratory at Johns Hopkins. In 1887, he founded the *American Journal of Psychology*, and in 1889 he became the first president of Clark University in Worcester, Massachusetts. Later, in 1892, he also contributed to the founding of the American Psychological Association.[35]

But his real claim to fame was twofold, one for his *magnum opus*, a ponderous two-volume study whose title clearly indicates the cosmic reach Wundt's successors intended to grasp: *Adolescence: Its Psychology and Its Relations to Physiology, Anthropology, Sociology, Sex, Crime, Religion, and Education*, and the other, his instrumental influence on the career of the one man whose name is associated with American education more than any other: John Dewey.[36] Dewey had studied for a year under Hall at Johns Hopkins, receiving his doctorate from that institution in 1884. By 1895, after a series of faculty appointments in the Universities of Minnesota and Michigan, Dewey joined the faculty "of the Rockefeller-endowed University of Chicago as head of the departments of philosophy, psychology, and pedagogy,"[37] where the University gave Dewey one thousand dollars to found "an education laboratory in which Dewey could apply psychological principles and experimental techniques to the study of learning."[38] It takes little imagination to guess just whose psychological principles operatively conditioned Dewey's "thinking" on education. More importantly, we now have the first indicators of what will become a consistent pattern, namely, the role of high finance capitalism in the sponsorship and promotion of such ideas. In Dewey, Wundtian behaviorism and its underlying mechanistic and materialistic cosmology, and finance capitalism in the form of the Rockefellers, find a common surface.

Dewey's philosophical impulses accurately reflect the fact that Wundt's basic principles and premises were being faithfully handed down:

> Education consists either in the ability to use one's powers in a social direction, or else in ability to share in the experiences of others and thus widen the individual consciousness to that of the race...[39]

---

34 Notably, Johns Hopkins, like many other American universities established during this time, was modeled along the lines of the German universities. See Lionni, *The Leipzig Connection*, p. 15.

35 Ibid., p. 15.

36 Ibid.

37 Ibid., p. 16.

38 Ibid., pp. 16–17.

39 John Dewey, *Lectures for the First Course in Pedagogy* (1896), unpublished, cited in Arthur G. Wirth, John Dewey as *Educator: His Design for Work in Education*

The First Wundtian Educational-Episcopal Succession:

WILHELM WUNDT, 1832–1920,
DOCTORAL MENTOR TO

G. STANLEY HALL, 1844–1924,
MENTOR TO

JOHN DEWEY, 1859–1952.

Note carefully that the implication of Dewey's comment is that education has been entirely redefined to being merely the activity of a "shared experience."

The importance of this conception can hardly be overestimated, for it implies in its turn that the role of a teacher has likewise been entirely redefined, from being that of a genuine educator to that of a "change agent" guiding "the socialization of the child, leading each youngster to *adapt* to the specific *behavior* required of him in order for him to *get along* in his group."[40] We would add yet another observation to Mr. Lionni's, a crucial one in fact, for what this sweeping and revolutionary redefinition of the teacher means is that the teacher's *real* role is one of designing appropriate stimulus-response-based "learning experiences,"[41] and for this, he or she needs to be trained as a kind of equivalent to the "paralegal"; the teacher becomes a kind of "parapsychologist" or "nurse practitioner" *requiring the special certification or credentialization authorizing them to apply psychological educational theory in the environs of the classroom.* It is this "competence" in designing "psychologically acceptable learning experiences"—according to the latest trendy theory—that forms the *real* basis behind the rise of the requirement for "teacher certification," for competence in specific academic disciplines such as literature or biology or music is no longer the main focus. The teacher becomes, in this analysis, the vicar for the far-off educational episcopacy and its theorists.

2. The Second Wundtian Succession: Wundt, Russell, Thorndike, and the Columbia Teachers College

This connection between the teacher-as-parapsychologist and learning-experience-designer is reinforced by yet another Wundtian succession, one leading directly to the founding of America's first "teacher certification" program, Columbia University's "Teachers College." Here one is confronted with two lines of succession that both lead directly to the Teachers College.

The first connection is via James Earl Russell, yet another of Wilhelm Wundt's students, who, having "received his doctorate from Leipzig in 1894, came to Columbia University in October, 1897."[42] Five years earlier,

---

(1894–1904) (New York: John Wiley & Sons, Inc., 1966), p. 28, cited in Paolo Lionni, *The Leipzig Connection*, p. 18.

40 Paolo Lionni, *The Leipzig Connection*, p. 19.

41 Ibid., p. 20.

42 Paolo Lionni, *The Leipzig Connection*, p. 26. Lionni also notes that during his

Columbia's Teachers College had been founded, and once Russell arrived, he was quickly appointed the dean of the college, establishing a department of "psychology and general method" within the college. There he would remain for "the next thirty years, building the largest institution in the world for the training of teachers."[43] As Lionni observes, with Russell's appointment at Columbia, Wundt's influence and doctrines were posed to metastasize throughout American education.[44]

The other Wundtian influence came from one of Russell's first hires at the Columbia Teachers College, Edward Lee Thorndike, who did his undergraduate studies "with Wundtians Armstrong and Judd,"[45] before continuing his graduate studies at Harvard under William James. During his studies at Harvard, Thorndike pioneered "animal psychology" by developing the "puzzle box," i.e., a labyrinth "into which he would put various animals (chickens, rats, cats) and let them find their way out by themselves."[46] Thorndike and his "puzzle box" came to the attention of yet another American Wundtian, James McKeen Cattell, who received his doctorate from Wundt and the University of Leipzig in 1886. Interestingly enough, Cattell's "primary interests lay in mental testing and in individual differences in ability."[47]

Nor was Cattell without his own uniquely deleterious effect and influence on American education:

> One series of experiments Cattell performed while at Leipzig examined the manner in which a person sees the words he is reading. Testing adults who knew how to read, Cattell found they could recognize words without having to sound out the letters. From this, he reasoned that words are not read by compounding the letters, but are perceived as "total word pictures."

However, from this insight, which seems perfectly normal to any literate adult, Cattell "deduced" in the sort of *non sequitur* typical of the "edugarchy"

...that little is gained by teaching the child his sounds and letters as the first

---

studies at Leipzig, Russell was also "an official European Agent for the Federal Bureau of Education (then located in the Department of the Interior)."

43 Ibid., pp. 26–27.

44 Ibid., p. 27.

45 Ibid., p. 30.

46 Paolo Lionni, *The Leipzig Connection*, p. 31.

47 Ibid., p. 21.

The Second Wundtian Educational-Episcopal Succession:

WILHELM WUNDT, 1832–1920,
DOCTORAL MENTOR TO

JAMES MCKEEN CATTELL, 1860–1944,   JAMES EARL RUSSELL, 1864–1945,
BOTH OF COLUMBIA TEACHERS COLLEGE, WHO HIRE

EDWARD LEE THORNDIKE, 1874–1949
(WHO ALSO DID UNDERGRADUATE STUDIES WITH WUNDTIANS ARMSTRONG AND JUDD)

step to being able to read. Since they could recognize words very rapidly, the way to teach children how to read would be to show them words, and tell them what the words were.[48]

This led to the "look-say" fad in reading pedagogy, for his findings "were subsequently applied by teachers trained in the new psychology, who managed to convert even this otherwise brilliant observation into a national crisis."[49]

In any case, it was Cattell who brought Thorndike and his "puzzle boxes" to the attention of Dean Russell of the Columbia Teachers College, who concluded that Thorndike's methods were worth exploring with respect to humans. Thorndike had applied for a fellowship at Columbia, which Cattell granted. Obtaining his Ph.D. there in 1898, Russell gave him a position at Teachers College, a position he occupied for thirty years.[50]

Thorndike, like other Wundtians, saw no purpose or value in traditional education. Rather, the school and its teachers were to be "change agents," and "socialization experience and activity facilitators," and he did not attempt to disguise his own views:

> Despite rapid progress in the right direction, the program of the average elementary school is too narrow and academic in character. Traditionally the elementary school has been primarily devoted to teaching the fundamental subjects, the three R's, and closely related disciplines... Artificial exercises, like drills on phonetics, multiplication tables, and formal writing movements, are used to a wasteful degree. Subjects such as arithmetic, language, and history include content that is intrinsically of little value.[51]

There one has it: traditional academic focus has little of intrinsic value; the only things of value are the socialization and collectivization "learning experiences and activities" of the teacher-practitioner of stimulus-response psychology.[52]

The result of this Wundtian "two-step"—step one being that man is an animal, and step two being that animals are complex stimulus-response

48 Ibid., p. 22.
49 Ibid., p. 23.
50 Paolo Lionni, *The Leipzig Connection*, p. 31.
51 Edward L. Thorndike and Arthur I. Gates, *Elementary Principles of Education* (New York: Macmillan, 1929), p. 308, cited in Paolo Lionni, *The Leipzig Connection*, p. 36.
52 Ibid., pp. 37–38.

machines—is a "society which operates more on the basis of gratification than on the basis of reason or responsibility,"[53] in which good grades or scores on standardized tests function within the overall stimulus-response educational culture as the rewards that lead to material gratification. Lionni quips, "the idea of rewarding a child for behaving like a human being would only occur to someone who supposes that the child is basically an animal and would have seemed like an open invitation to blackmail to any sensible 19th-century parent."[54]

And what of James McKeen Cattell, who first brought Thorndike to Columbia and then to the attention of the Dean of the Teachers College, James Earl Russell? Interestingly enough, in 1887 he journeyed to Cambridge University in Great Britain to deliver a series of lectures. There, Cattell met Charles Darwin's cousin, the British psychologist and eugenics theorist Francis Galton, and

> ...quickly absorbed Galton's approach to eugenics, selective breeding, and the measurement of intelligence. Cattell was later to become the American leader in psychological testing, and in 1894 would administer the first battery of psychological tests ever given to a large group of people, testing the freshman and senior classes at Columbia University.[55]

In other words, standardized tests were viewed as part of the sorting mechanism that the socialization processes of "progressive" education envisioned,

---

53 Ibid., p. 34.

54 Ibid., p. 35. It is worth noting that Thorndike adopts the stimulus-response approach to the psychologizing of teaching in a total sense. In his 1906 book *The Principles of Teaching Based on Psychology*, he defines teaching as "...the art of giving and withholding stimuli with the result of producing or preventing certain responses. In this definition the term stimulus is used widely for any event which influences a person—for a word spoken to him, a look, a sentence which he reads, the air he breathes, etc., etc. The term response is used for any reaction made by him—a new thought, a feeling of interest, a bodily act, any mental or bodily condition resulting from the stimulus. The aim of the teacher is to produce desirable and prevent undesirable changes in human beings by producing and preventing certain responses. The means at the disposal of the teacher are the stimuli which can be brought to bear upon the pupil—the teacher's words, gestures, and appearance, the condition and appliances of the school room, the books to be used and the objects to be seen, and so on through a long list of the things and events which the teacher can control." (Charlotte Thomson Iserbyt, *The Deliberate Dumbing Down of America: A Chronological Paper Trail*, Revised and Abridged Edition [Parlman, OH: Conscience Press, 2001], p. 21.)

55 Paolo Lionni, *The Leipzig Connection*, p. 23.

a point worth keeping in mind, since the real rot at the heart of Common Core *is the individually tailored computerized standard tests that will track, follow, and* **sort** *students throughout the entire public "education" process.*

GEORGE S. COUNTS, PH.D. (1889–1974),
PH.D. FROM THE UNIVERSITY OF CHICAGO, 1916,
PROFESSOR, COLUMBIA UNIVERSITY TEACHERS COLLEGE, 1927–1955

3. The First Wundtian Succession Again, and George S. Counts

One of John Dewey's, and therefore the first "succession's" most influential, students was George Sylvester Counts (1889–1974), a leader in the formation of teachers' unions, and eventually a critic of the Dewey wing of the progressive education movement. For Counts, the progressive education movement did not go far *enough*. Indeed, "In *The Selective Character of American Secondary Education* (1922), he documented the failure of the public high school to reduce significantly the unequal distribution of wealth and privilege in American society,"[56] and in other similar studies Counts concluded "that the school was one of many American institutions that did not work for the ordinary citizen but functioned instead to maintain class distinctions...".[57] Consequently, Counts

---

56 Wayne J. Urban, "Preface" to George S. Counts, *Dare the School Build a New Social Order?* (Carbondale, IL: Southern Illinois University Press, Arcturus Books, 1978), p. vii.

57 Ibid.

viewed the educational changes inside Stalin's Russia in a favorable light, since like all "progressive" educators in the Wundtian succession, he viewed education as a laboratory for the creation of social change, and for the study of its results.[58] Not surprisingly, Counts maintained that teachers (and hence schools) not only were "change agents" but were the primary change agents, and should view themselves, and be viewed, as such.[59] Counts comes to this position because, in his words, "on all genuinely crucial matters the school follows the wishes of the groups or classes that actually rule society…".[60]

But like other Wundtians, Counts also views the child as a machine and a *tabula rasa*,[61] for whom a set of learning experiences, *coupled with indoctrination in appropriately "democratic" ideals as defined by progressives*,[62] is paramount. "If the machine is to serve all," he states, "and serve all equally, it cannot be the property of the few."[63]

With Counts, one comes face to face with the inherent dialectical conflict within the educational system, a dialectic whose polar opposites he himself characterizes as that between "feudalism" with its hierarchical order and class distinctions, and democracy.[64] We have seen, too, the subtle suggestions that standardized testing is both an implicit *leveler* to the "lowest common denominator," and yet at the same time subtle suggestions—as in the case of Cattell—that it was also envisioned as a sorting mechanism to establish the credentials of an "aristocracy of nature and merit" rather than one of heredity, of those "gifted with the right to govern." Is there any way to reconcile these two seemingly opposed trends within the Wundtian succession?

Indeed there is, but for that, we shall have to probe more deeply into the historical manifestation of that systemic dialectic, into its architects, and into why they erected such a system.

---

58 Wayne J. Urban, "Preface" to George S. Counts, *Dare the School Build a New Social Order?*, p. viii. Needless to say, as Urban points out, such views made Counts an extremely controversial figure, and many accused him of being a Communist, in spite of the fact that he never joined the American Communist Party, and in spite of the fact that "In the 1930s and 1940s, he led a battle to expel the communists—because of their totalitarianism—from the American Federation of Teachers." (p. viii)

59 George S. Counts, *Dare the School Build a New Social Order?*, pp. x–xi, 28.

60 Ibid., p. 25.

61 Ibid., p. 13.

62 Ibid., p. 7.

63 Ibid., p. 41.

64 Ibid.

The "Edugarchy"
Standardized Testing and the Cosmology
of the Global Skinner Box

"Conant... had a plan fully worked out, which he had recently proposed in a series of righteous, almost inflammatory magazine articles: to depose the existing, undemocratic American elite and replace it with a new one made up of brainy, elaborately trained, public-spirited people drawn from every section and every background."

—

NICHOLAS LEMANN[1]

"We violate the child's nature and render difficult the best ethical results by introducing the child too abruptly to a number of special studies, or reading, writing, geography, etc. out of relation to his social life... the true center of correlation of the school subjects is not science, nor literature, nor history, nor geography, but the child's own social activities."

—

JOHN DEWEY[2]

I f the truth be told, the dialectical dilemma between the "feudalism" and hierarchical organization of the American elite and education on the one hand, and the "democratic" and "leveling" impulse of the progressives like Counts on the other, was never solved, at least not in any sense that would be obvious to a passerby looking at the phenomenon.

---

1   Nicholas Lemann, *The Big Test: The Secret History of the American Meritocracy* (New York: Farrar, Straus and Giroux, 1999), p. 5.
2   Martin S. Dworkin, ed., *Dewey on Education: Selections* (New York: Columbia University Teachers College, 1975), p. 25.

Only when one digs deeply into it does one discover an ingenious fusion of the two, one designed ultimately to create a sorting mechanism, via education and standardized tests, which would slot people into the most acceptable "career" for their lives, while identifying the "most gifted" few for promotion and inclusion in the ranks of the power elite.

There is, however, an inherent danger in this plan, and it is one that one of your authors—Joseph Farrell—has pointed out from time to time in various public forums and interviews, and it is also one that the careful reader will have caught: if everyone in the USA was subjected to a regimen of standardized tests, based on "progressive" educational theories that were in their turn ultimately based on the theories of Wilhelm Wundt and his successors, and if these standardized tests display every indication of being written to *punish* the most intellectually gifted or well-informed test-takers, then the ultimate effect will be a dumbing-down of the elite itself.

This will afford our point of entry into the difficult territory of negotiating the contradictory impulses at work in American education, and why that contradiction was deliberately engineered into the system, for this consideration brings us chin-to-chin with:

A. The Dumbed-Down Elites and Quackery at the Heart of Quackademia: Abraham Flexner, the Rockefeller General Education Board, and the Lincoln School

The key figure here is Abraham Flexner (1866–1959), for he demonstrates in a quite unique fashion the "Germanization" of American education, the common surface or interface between the "edugarchy" and the financial elite via their various foundations, and the pervasive dumbing down of the financial-power elite itself. It was Flexner, in fact, who founded the Institute of Advanced Study at Princeton University, presiding over it from 1930–1939.[3]

---

3 As the Wikipedia article notes, Flexner's tenure as the head of the Institute for Advanced Study would have put him in charge of a very eminent faculty, one including the famous mathematician Kurt Gödel, and information-theorist and mathematician John von Neumann. Flexner was instrumental in bringing Albert Einstein to the Institute, having composed the formal letter of invitation to him.

ABRAHAM FLEXNER

For our purposes of the moment, however, Flexner is to be remembered for the twin influences he had on both American medicine and on American education. Flexner graduated with an undergraduate degree from Johns Hopkins—a university which, as we have seen, was rife with Wundtian influences—and later pursued, though never completed, graduate work at the University of Berlin, one-time home to the renowned German idealist philosopher Georg Friedrich Wilhelm Hegel. Thus, unlike many principals in this historical drama, Flexner did not have any direct connections to the "Wundtian succession" other than its influences at Johns Hopkins.[4]

Returning from Germany without having completed his graduate degree, Flexner decided to test his theories of education by opening a college preparatory school in his hometown of Louisville, Kentucky. This brought him to the attention of powerful financial interests, and he eventually joined the Carnegie Foundation for the Advancement of Teaching doing research on the American, English, and German college and university systems, a post which he left in 1913 to go to work as assistant secretary for the Rockefellers' General Education Board.[5]

---

4   Paolo Lionni, *The Leipzig Connectionn*, p. 68.
5   Ibid.

1. Flexner and the Beginning of "Allopathic" Medicine

Like many American educational theorists of the time, Flexner was bewitched by the rigorous German system of secondary and university education. Indeed, it was during his tenure as a researcher for the Carnegie Foundation that he was tasked with studying medical school conditions in the United States and Canada, which he did by conducting an eighteen-month-long tour and study of over 150 Canadian and American medical colleges.[6] The Carnegie Foundation subsequently sent Flexner on a European tour "to survey the medical schools in England, Scotland, France, Germany, and Austria."[7] The Carnegie Foundation, however, ultimately proved inhospitable to his theories, and Flexner left it to join the Rockefeller family's General Education Board in 1913.

It is here that one finds the beginnings, not only of the dumbing down of America's youth, but of their "drugging down" as well:

> By the time Flexner joined the Board, his attack on American medical education, which had been front-page news across the country, had resulted in the number of medical schools in the United States dropping from 147 to 95. Naturopathic medicine was on the decline in this country, as it was proving particularly unsusceptible to Rockefeller funding. Over the years (until 1960), the General Education Board would give a total of over $96 million to medical schools which, like Johns Hopkins, disregarded naturopathy, homeopathy, and chiropractic in favor of medicine based on the use of surgery and chemical drugs. The Board's sponsorship of chemical medicine on the one hand and psychology on the other would culminate in 1963 when a group of researchers at Johns Hopkins developed the use of Ritalin to "treat" children who were regarded as "troubled" or too active.[8]

In effect, what Flexner had accomplished was a truly occult magical working, though he and others of the time would hardly have perceived it as such, for he accomplished the "alchemical wedding" of Wundtian psychological theories and German-style "chemical medicine" in American education, transforming it into an effective form of soft mind control and social engineering, for the alchemical transformation of man.[9]

---

6   Ibid., p. 69.
7   Ibid., p. 70.
8   Paolo Lionni, *The Leipzig Connection*, p. 71.
9   Ibid., pp. 71–72.

2. Flexner's Lincoln School: Dumbing Down the Elite Themselves

But Flexner was not done. In 1916, while at the Rockefeller General Education Board and under its aegis and imprint, he published a controversial paper innocuously titled "A Modern School." Its contents, however, were anything but innocent or innocuous, for in it he proposed an experimental school which would abolish the study of Greek and Latin, and under which literature and history "would not be completely abolished, but new methods would be instituted for teaching these subjects."[10] Additionally, the study of classical literature and English grammar would be completely dropped.[11]

In other words, Flexner's program amounted to nothing less than a *total* program to *sever* American education and students from an informed understanding of their roots within Western culture; it was a program designed to *rob* them of their culture, and hence, of their critical and independent reasoning faculties. Even *The New York Times* chimed in on what the real underlying philosophy of Flexner's proposal really was, and what its ultimate issue would be:

> Unblushing materialism finds its crowning triumph in the theory of the modern school. *In the whole plane there is not a spiritual thought, not an idea that rises about the need of finding money for the pocket and food for the belly...* It is a matter of instant inquiry, for very sober consideration, whether the General Education Board, indeed, may not with the immense funds at its disposal be able to shape to its will practically all the institutions in which the youth of the country are trained.
>
> If this experiment bears the expected fruit we shall see imposed on the country a system of education born of the theories of one or two men, and replacing a system which has been the natural outgrowth of the American character and the needs of the American people...[12]

It takes little reading between the lines to see what the agenda was, for it was nothing less than to produce a completely materialist, narcissistic society of wants and gratifications, of stimuli and responses, a consumerist society with little grounding in the spiritual roots of its cultural past, nor with any deep

---

10 Ibid., p. 72.

11 Paolo Lionni, *The Leipzig Connection*, p. 72.

12 *The New York Times*, January 21, 1917, Sections 7–8, p. 2, cited in Lionni, *The Leipzig Connection*, p. 74, our emphasis.

long-term appreciation of the future nor of the consequences of unbridled consumerism. It was to produce a society living only in the ever-present "now," with all its wants and needs. To effect that, education had to give the general public *just enough* education to effect its transformation into good consumers, but *not* enough to question the philosophical assumptions it was putting into place.[13]

While the debate over "The Modern School" was quite public and vigorous, America's entry into World War I in April of 1917 served to distract the nation, while the War itself provided the "crisis of opportunity" for the educational progressives to begin their march through the institutions, as we shall discover subsequently in this chapter. That march has proceeded more or less unimpeded down to its current manifestation in the assessment process of Common Core, and thus it is important to see how that march was conducted, how its strategies, tactics, and alliances were formed.

One gains a measure of at least some of those tactics in the next step undertaken by Flexner to implement his theories. Flexner, now connected to the other major disseminator of Wundtian influence in the USA, Columbia's Teachers College, decided to combine forces with it and introduce Columbia's long-sought "laboratory school"—note the terminology—in the form of his own proposals in "The Modern School," using a million and a half dollars

---

13   *The New York Times* was not the only national organ to complain about "progressive" education and its financial backers. According to the well-known Reagan Administration "defector" from the U.S. Department of Education (the department that Reagan promised to abolish but didn't), Charlotte Thomson Iserbyt, the National Education Association itself, during its 1914 annual meeting in St. Paul, Minnesota, registered extreme concern about the educational activities of the Carnegie and Rockefeller Foundations in a resolution, which stated in part: "We view with alarm the activity of the Carnegie and Rockefeller Foundations— agencies not in any way responsible to the people—in their efforts to control the policies of our State educational institutions, to fashion after their conception and to standardize our courses of study, and to surround the institutions with conditions which menace true academic freedom and defeat the primary purpose of democracy as heretofore preserved inviolate in our common schools, normal schools, and universities." (Charlotte Thomson Iserbyt, *The Deliberate Dumbing Down of America: A Chronological Paper Trail*, Revised and Abridged Edition [Parkman, OH: Conscience Press, 2001], p. 27.) For those unaware of the wider story, it was Charlotte Thomson Iserbyt who supplied the bound volume of the Skull and Bones Society's annual membership list—her father having been an initiate—to former Hoover Institute Fellow and history scholar, Anthony Sutton, who used the materials to write one of his most controversial books, *America's Secret Establishment: An Introduction to the Order of Skull and Bones.*

of the Rockefeller General Education Board's money to do it. So vociferous had been the debate, however, over his proposals in "The Modern School," that the decision was taken to name it not "The Modern Laboratory School," thereby openly proclaiming its relationship to Flexner, but rather to name it "The Lincoln School."[14] With this, one sees what will become a familiar tactic: an appeal to patriotism to support ideas in radical opposition to the fundamental tenets of Western culture as realized in the American republic. It is, in effect, the old Gnostic tactic of using the terms of "orthodoxy" (in this case political and cultural orthodoxy) to cloak a revolutionary agenda completely counter to it.

But what happened next not even the progressive educators had dared guess nor hope for: "John D. Rockefeller, Jr., sent four of his five sons to study at the Lincoln School, with results that could, perhaps, have been predicted had he read the works of Thorndike and Dewey,"[15] for Laurance Rockefeller would later complain that he could not read and write to the level he wished, while Nelson Aldrich, later U.S. intelligence officer during World War II for Latin America, subsequent advisor to President Eisenhower on national security policy, and later governor of New York and Vice President, would complain that reading was not something he enjoyed, but rather that he found to be "a slow and torturous process."[16]

Thus the financial elite itself, perhaps anxious to reassure the country that the sauce for the middle-class goose was good enough sauce for the upper-class gander, had fallen prey to its own experts, and succeeded in dumbing down its own progeny! This pattern of foundation money, not-too-bright busybody billionaires, and Wundtian-style stimulus-response psychologizing of education we shall encounter again and again, all the way up to its current manifestation in the advocacy for the Common Core program.

Nor is our observation about the ultimate goal—the transformation of society and culture into one whose sole basis is a kind of passive materialism, narcissism, and consumerism—wide of the mark, for in the views of Dewey disciple and Columbia Teachers College professor Harold Rugg, yet another name in the long line of the Wundtian succession, education was to be a soft component of *an entirely new type and system of governance,* surrounding the

---

14 Paolo Lionni, *The Leipzig Connection,* pp. 78–79.

15 Ibid., p. 79.

16 Paolo Lionni, *The Leipzig Connection,* p. 80, citing Jules Abels, *The Rockefeller Billions: The Story of the World's Most Stupendous Fortune* (New York: Macmillan, 1965), p. 343.

individual in a variety of coordinated "activities" designed ultimately for total economic coordination, including the "production of a new race of educational workers."[17] The school, in other words, was not an institution for the transmission of a cultural and academic tradition, but was rather to be viewed principally as a mechanism of social engineering and indoctrination precisely in order to *disconnect* the great mass of people from their cultural heritage.

B. Conant, Chauncey, and the Testing Theocracy
1. Education for "World Citizenship"

That the school was to be transformed into a mechanism, not of education, but of social and cultural engineering as a "soft" form of mind manipulation and as a component of a new system of governance, was revealed by the Progressive Education Association in its board meeting held from November 15–17, 1943, in Chicago. Founded by Wundtian John Dewey in 1919, the Progressive Education Association's board issued a statement based on its deliberations at that meeting, and published it in its December 1943 issue of its own *Progressive Education.* The statement is revealing of this wider political purpose:

> This is a global war, and the peace now in the making will determine what our national life will be for the next century. It will demonstrate the degree of our national morality. *We are writing now the credo by which our children* **must** *live.*
>
> Your Board unanimously proposes a broadening of the interests and program of this Association to include the communities in which our children live. To this end, they propose additions to the governing body to include representatives of welfare services, health, industry, labor and the professions. In short, a cross-section body to give scope to our program....
>
> Yes, something happened around a table in Chicago. An organization

---

17 Harold Rugg, *The Great Technology, Social Chaos, and the Public Mind* (1933), p. 258. Rugg was yet another educator in the Progressive-Wundtian conceptual succession, and, more than most, was unequivocal in his statements that education was to be a tool of social engineering and hence of a "new conception of government," for it was "through the schools of the world we shall disseminate a new conception of government—one that will embrace all of the collective activities of men; one that will postulate the need for scientific control and operation of economic activities in the interests of all people." (Ibid., p. 271)

which might have become mellowed with the years to futility, in three short days *again drew a blueprint for children of the world.*[18]

The language of the statement is revealing, from the imperative mood of "the credo by which our children *must* live" to the treatment of education, and children, as a sort of mechanized architectural "project" or "blueprint," nor is that "blueprint" restricted to American children, but rather, the "credo" by which future generations *must* live is a blueprint for a *global* system, "for the children of the world."

Nor was the Progressive Education Association alone in its demands for a "global" schooling system to indoctrinate coming generations in the new globalist creed. In 1943, the American Federation of Teachers published a book authored in part by George S. Counts, titled *America, Russia, and the Communist Party in the Postwar World*. In its Preface, the book indicates that one of the problems "progressive" education must face is that of "education for world-citizenship."[19]

All of these studies reflected a *prewar* study, funded by the Carnegie Corporation in 1934, a study which was eventually published in the book *Conclusions and Recommendations for the Social Studies*, under the auspices of the American Historical Association. The significant implications of this sponsorship are revealed by a significant statement on the very first page:

> The Commission could not limit itself to a survey of textbooks, curricula, methods of instruction, and schemes of examination, but was impelled to consider the condition and prospects of the American people *as a part of Western Civilization merging into a world order.*[20]

In other words, the American Historical Association viewed, and views, its role principally as a "gatekeeper" insuring that curricula, textbooks, and pedagogy are all consonant to "a world order." Those components of Western civilization that are *not* consonant to that order are presumably to be ignored and gradually withdrawn from the popular culture via the social engineering process of schooling.

---

18 Charlotte Thomson Iserbyt, *The Dumbing Down of America*, p. 28, citing Progressive Education, December 1943, Vol. XX, No. 8. Our boldface and italicized emphasis.

19 Charlotte Thomson Iserbyt, *The Dumbing Down of America*, p. 50.

20 Ibid., p. 40, citing the American Historical Association, *Conclusions and Recommendations of the Social Studies* (New York: Chas. Scribner's Sons, 1934), p. 1.

This was not, however, the only book published under the auspices of the American Historical Association with Carnegie Corporation money in 1934, for in that same year, Ernest Horn published *Methods of Instruction in the Social Studies*, the fifteenth part of the American Historical Association's *Report of the Commission on the Social Studies*. In the preface to this volume, written by the Chairman of the Commission, A.C. Krey, the first paragraph is starkly revealing of yet another agenda:

> To teachers, **methods of instruction rank with the curriculum as matters of most immediate concern.** The two are closely related; and though the Commission sought at first to deal with each separately, it soon found it desirable to appoint an advisory committee to consider them together. This committee canvassed the possibility of conducting extensive experiments to determine the relative effectiveness of the various methods of instruction used in the social studies. The complexity of the teaching procedures, *the lack of adequate objective measures as well as the difficulties in conducting controlled experiments* which could be at all convincing deterred the committee from any extensive efforts in this direction.[21]

Note that Krey complains of the "lack of adequate objective measures" in conjunction with "the difficulties in conducting controlled experiments." In other words, the progressive educators were seeking an "objective" tool by which they could measure the relative success of their programs over time. But the tool, the standardized test, was already there; what they were *really* seeking was a way to inject the viral cancer into the system, so that it would rapidly metastasize.

2. Henry Chauncey and the "Census of Abilities"

More than any other individual in this story of the "edugarchy" and testing episcopate, it is Henry Chauncey (1905–2002) who, along with James Bryant Conant, grafted the standardized test onto the progressive education philosophy that was marching through the institutions of American education.

---

21 A.C. Krey, "Preface," in Ernest Horn, *Methods of Instruction in the Social Studies, Part XV: Report of the Commission on the Social Studies, American Historical Association* (New York: Charles Scribner's Sons, 1934), p. vii, bold-italics emphasis added.

HENRY CHAUNCEY, 1905–2002,
FOUNDER OF THE EDUCATION TESTING SERVICE,
PRINCETON, NEW JERSEY, 1947

Chauncey, the son of an Episcopal priest and an alumnus of one of the country's most prestigious Episcopalian boarding schools,[22] had a vision one Sunday morning in church, or rather, since he was Episcopalian, perhaps it is better to say that he had an "epiphany."

Chauncey's epiphany was nothing less than to take the standardized tests that had begun to be administered on a mass basis in the U.S. military during World War I[23] as a means to determine quickly which draftees were capable of promotion to officers, and which were not, and institute the same program on a nationwide basis to determine who was "college material" and who was not. He called it a "census of abilities" and even referred to it as "a census of our human resources in terms of capacities for different kinds of employment."[24] In this goal, he was joined by those who called for a massive expansion of the public education system, an expansion that occurred in part due to the economic pressures of the Great Depression, as we have seen.

---

22 Nicholas Lemann, *The Big Test: The Secret History of the American Meritocracy* (New York: Farrar, Straus and Giroux, 1999), p. 3. We heartily recommend this book to anyone wanting a quick, readable, but detailed overview of the history of standardized testing.

23 Ibid., pp. 23–24.

24 Ibid., pp. 4–5.

One of those who called for such expansion, and who wanted to see the "hereditary oligarchical" structure of the Eastern Establishment, with its easy access to the Ivy League universities, replaced by a "natural aristocracy" led by "people of ability," was precisely Chauncey's boss at Harvard University, its president, James Bryant Conant.[25] The problem, of course, was how to find and identify such persons.

Enter Henry Chauncey and his "census of abilities."

Chauncey's "epiphany" occurred during the time that there were basically four fundamental ideas competing for the future of American education. The first—the Wundtian educational succession and its wealthy foundation backers—we have already encountered. The second idea, equally promoted by such wealthy patrons as the Carnegie Foundation, was that of the imposition of a uniform standard of curriculum and assessment on schools, the idea being to establish a body of material "that all students in high school and college should be required to master, test them on it, and ruthlessly weed out the student population on the basis of the test results."[26] This finding was a result of an eight-year study funded by the Carnegie Foundation and conducted under the auspices of the Progressive Education Association in the 1920s and 1930s.

The third idea, of course, was that if one wished to *have* such a "common core" curriculum, and a common basis of evaluation, one had to have something like Henry Chauncey's "census of abilities," a standardized test to be administered to all American students, and evaluated by certain uniform standards. The fourth competing idea was that *everyone* should have some form of education—be it academic or vocational—all the way through high school, and hence, the entire system had to be massively expanded.[27]

3. A Coup d'État via Social Engineering and Standardized Testing

Chauncey's "census of abilities" obviously had utility to each camp; it was the *one* thing—insofar as the camps were *disagreed* with each other (or pretended to be)—that they could agree upon, for no matter what approach one took,

---

25 Lemann, *The Big Test*, p. 8. See also Lemann's discussion on pp. 41–44, 47, 52, for the Jeffersonian influence on Conant's idea of a natural aristocracy, or meritocracy.

26 Lemann, *The Big Test*, pp. 22–23.

27 For Lemann's discussion of these four competing philosophies, see pp. 21–23.

"the one thing they all had in common" was that "they all involved more testing."[28] His project, in other words, amounts to nothing less than "a vast scientific project that will categorize, sort, and route the entire population"[29] via the administration of the now-familiar standardized multiple-choice test, whose scores amount to "suggestions" of what each person's optimal vocation or career should be. It was, in the words of Nicholas Lemann, "an audacious plan for engineering a change in the leadership group and social structure of the country—a kind of quiet, planned coup d'état."[30] Testing, in other words, as we have observed before, was to become an integral component of the structure of governance and a crucial tool in the arsenal of social engineering.

The first stage in the implementation of this scheme came in the 1930s, when Conant decided to implement a new series of scholarships to Harvard that would be available to anyone, from anywhere in the country and from any background or class, not just the traditional Eastern Establishment. For poor students, the scholarships would be a full four-year grant, with all tuition, room and board, covered. For students from wealthier classes able to pay, the scholarships would nonetheless be awarded, but without the money. In this way Conant sought to cloak the scholarships with an aura of elite status, since the real basis of their award was to be solely on the basis of academic performance.[31]

Conant wanted to ensure that his scholarship candidates performed well during their stay at Harvard, and to this end he needed a new admissions test that would give "objective" results and which could be "objectively" evaluated, replacing the old College Entrance Examination Board's essay tests. He and Chauncey turned to one Carl Campbell Brigham, a psychologist, a professor, and the creator of a standardized intelligence and aptitude test called the Scholastic Aptitude Test.[32]

4. The First Dirty Little Secret:
The Designer of the SAT was a Eugenicist

Not surprisingly, Brigham "was an ardent eugenicist,"[33] and viewed testing as a means whereby "the good stock" could be sorted out from "the bad

---

28 Lemann, *The Big Test*, p. 26.
29 Ibid., p. 5.
30 Ibid., p. 6.
31 Ibid., p. 28.
32 Ibid., pp. 28–29.
33 Lemann, *The Big Test*, p. 29.

stock." Brigham even authored a book, *A Study of American Intelligence*, in which he peddled the then-prevailing eugenicist theory that "there were three distinct white races in Europe—in descending order of intelligence, Nordic, Alpine, and Mediterranean... ."[34] The Army intelligence tests, given *en masse* to draftees during World War I, not surprisingly "confirmed" these views.[35] In Brigham's hands, these tests "metamorphosed into the SAT"[36] by 1926, for on June 23, 1926, the SAT was administered for the first time to a group of over 8,000 high school students in the Northeast. The U.S. Army also allowed Brigham to administer the test to its West Point applicants, and by 1930 the U.S. Navy followed suit and allowed Brigham to give the test to its Naval Academy candidates at Annapolis.[37]

There was a fly in the ointment, however, and it was Brigham himself, who began to question not only the efficacy of his test, but also its underlying assumptions. Initially, the SAT score was one number, and Brigham himself made the connection between its score and its claims to measure "intelligence" by publishing a "conversion" scale for "converting the SAT score into an IQ score."[38] Eventually, however, Brigham was persuaded "to divide the SAT score into two parts, one for verbal and one for mathematical ability"[39] and to give up the idea of a "conversion scale" which would connect the SAT implicitly to the idea that it could measure intelligence. Eventually, even this was not satisfactory to Brigham, who in a 1929 letter to his friend and fellow eugenicist Charles Davenport stated that testing advocates should stop making any claim whatsoever of what such tests measured, calling such claims "psycho-phrenology."[40] By 1934, Brigham had reversed his position almost entirely, claiming that such tests were incapable of measuring "native intelligence" and that any score was based on a combination of factors, including the individual's schooling, fluency in English, social class, family background, and a variety of other hidden factors.[41] Chauncey, Conant, and the emerging testing "edugarchy" were by this point deaf to any critiques, since the standardized test was so readily adaptable to their social engineering agenda.

---

34 Ibid., p. 30.
35 Ibid.
36 Ibid., p. 31.
37 Ibid., p. 32.
38 Ibid., p. 33.
39 Ibid.
40 Lemann, *The Big Test*, p. 33.
41 Ibid., p. 34.

5. The Invention of the Markograph and Computerized "Objective" Evaluation, and the Emergence of the Educational-Industrial Complex

The next stage in the emergence of Chauncey's dream was afforded by the invention, in 1931, of an automated grading machine called a "Markograph" by a Michigan high school science teacher, Reynold B. Johnson. Noting that lead conducts electricity, Johnson designed answer sheets to multiple-choice examinations that have become the now familiar "bubble test" computerized answer sheets. IBM, which had sought to develop its own testing-grading machine since 1928, bought the rights to Johnson's Markograph,[42] and by 1936, IBM machines, descendants of the Markograph, were being used in New York and Rhode Island for the first mass-mechanized "evaluations" of standardized testing. As Lemann quips, mass testing "was now technically feasible."[43]

It was also becoming big business, regardless of the efficacy of the tests themselves, or the validity of their underlying assumptions. By the late 1930s, as the SAT and other such standardized tests were increasingly in use to determine "aptitude for college," James Bryant Conant took the next step, and publicly proposed "that a new national testing agency be created to operate all the leading standardized educational tests...."[44]

Conant's public calls for such an agency did not go without challenge, however. And the challenge came from no less than Carl Brigham, the "inventor" of the SAT himself! Brigham complained that if such an agency were established, and hence with it the idea of the utility of nationalized standardized testing, that *education would become confused with test results* to the point that "any organization that owned the rights to a particular test would inevitably become more interested in promoting it than in honestly evaluating its effectiveness."[45] It was, Brigham complained, "probably simpler to teach cultured men testing than to give testers culture."[46]

---

42 Ibid., p. 37.

43 Ibid., p. 38. Lemann also notes that Ralph Waldo Emerson, himself a proponent of the Jeffersonian ideal of a "natural aristocracy of merit," dreamed of an "anthropometer" that would be able to measure each individual's relative "merit" and suitability for "rule." Conant, he observes, had in Brigham's SAT and the emerging mechanized "evaluation" technology, "the anthropometer that Emerson dreamed of." (p. 45)

44 Lemann, *The Big Test*, pp. 39–40.

45 Ibid., p. 40.

46 Ibid. Brigham's comments appeared in an article published in the educational magazine *School and Society* in December 1937 (p. 40).

By early 1938, Brigham wrote a letter to Conant himself, and spelled out the ultimate consequences of the standardized testing folly, and the even more egregious folly of making national institutions and testing agencies to administer them:

> If the unhappy day ever comes when teachers point their students toward these newer examinations, and the present weak and restricted procedures get a grip on education, then we may look for the inevitable distortion of education in terms of tests. And that means that mathematics will continue to be completely departmentalized and broken into disintegrated bits, that the sciences will become highly verbalized and that computation, manipulation and thinking in terms other than verbal will be minimized, that languages will be taught for linguistic skills only without reference to literary values, that English will be taught for reading alone, and that practice and drill in the writing of English will disappear.[47]

These criticisms—as true of Common Core's mysterious evaluation process now as they were of standardized tests back then—fell on deaf ears, for in the aftermath of World War II (and after much behind-the-scenes maneuvering, including some pressure from the Carnegie Foundation against rival tests and testing schemes)[48] Henry Chauncey's Educational Testing Service was chartered, and opened for business on January 1, 1948.[49]

That the "edugarchy" intended testing to be a tool of social engineering and governance is revealed by the fact that, in 1948, both President Truman and James Bryant Conant were in favor of a universal compulsory military *training*, a kind of Americanized *Dienstpflicht*.[50] Congress would have none of it, and opted only for a universal draft registration. There was a loophole, and that was that the new "natural aristocracy" that Conant and Chauncey were seeking to create had to be protected from this draft, and that led to the creation of draft-deferment testing.[51] With the North Korean invasion of South Korea in 1950, Chauncey's Educational Testing Service had to create,

---

47 Lemann, *The Big Test*, pp. 40–41.

48 Ibid., p. 63.

49 Ibid., p. 54. Lemann notes that Chauncey "later thought he might have chosen the name" Educational Testing Service "because it echoed that of his father's alma mater, the Episcopal Theological Seminary." (p. 65)

50 Ibid., p. 72.

51 Ibid., pp. 72–73.

and administer, the new test, a test that was "quite literally a matter of life and death."[52]

Lemann observes that the social engineering scheme of testing as a sorting mechanism began to come under fire in newspapers around the country. For example, "The editorial cartoonist of *The Sacramento Bee* drew Joseph Stalin walking into his propaganda department, wearing a self-satisfied grin and holding a piece of paper that said: 'PRESIDENT TRUMAN ADVOCATES DRAFT DEFERMENT FOR COLLEGE BOYS—U.S. TO INITIATE CASTE SYSTEM.'"[53] Through Chauncey's careful politicking and advocacy, however, the country came to accept the draft deferment test, and with it the idea of mass standardized testing in general. After all, it was far cheaper as a sorting mechanism to institutions required "to process large numbers of people quickly," than universal military service.[54]

But the draft deferment test issue forced Chauncey's Educational Testing Service to admit that it was a huge instrument of the soft power of governance, and a tool of social engineering:

> During the Korean crisis the findings of Educational Testing Service played what was in many cases a life and death role, since it was called upon to determine which young men should be permitted to continue their educations and which inducted into military service.... As an institution of national scope dealing in the guidance of human lives, it has no close parallel in our society. Under the circumstances it is well to remember that the idea of any center of power, perhaps particularly one which classifies people, is historically viewed with misgivings by Americans. It has gotten both governmental and private institutions into trouble again and again.[55]

Such sentiments reflected the views of ETS' founder, Henry Chauncey, and his powerful patron, James Bryant Conant.

Not content with merely measuring "scholastic aptitude," Chauncey was constantly on the lookout for other tests, including tests that could measure and classify such imponderables as "persistence" and "personality" and

---

52 Ibid., p. 75.
53 Ibid.
54 Lemann, *The Big Test*, p. 87.
55 Ibid., pp. 79–80. Caveat lector: It should be noted that Lemann provides no bibliographical information for the source of this quotation, nor when nor in what context it was made.

even aptitude for espionage![56] And he minced no words concerning his own perceptions of the power that standardized testing would give its purveyors, writing in his diary that "What I hope to see established... is the moral equivalent of religion but based on reason and science rather than on sentiments and tradition."[57] And testing was the key:

> "We seem... to have arrived at the period in Man's history when human affairs can be studied as impartially and scientifically as physical phenomena," he wrote in his diary.

And with that statement, we are bold to point out its strong philosophical resemblance to the assumptions of Wilhelm Wundt. Lemann comments on what we are calling Chauncey's and standardized testing's "Wundtian impulse," as follows:

> Just as the Manhattan Project had split the atom, the Educational Testing Service, with its research department made up of the best minds in the field, would decode the mind. Many more people than just aspiring college and graduate students would be tested, and for many more qualities. ETS would measure all abilities, not just aptitude or intelligence. It would map and code the personality. This new knowledge would help human affairs to take on a new conformation: rational understanding would replace prejudice, hatred, emotion, and superstition. Human nature itself would be reformed.[58]

Or, as Lemann puts it elsewhere:

> Only one problem consistently gnawed at Henry Chauncey as he ran ETS and that was the narrowness of what the ETS tests measured and of the use to which the scores were put. He had agreed to run ETS because he thought mental testing was a scientific miracle that would soon reveal all the ancient mysteries of the mind, and as soon as it did, he wanted to mount the Census of Abilities—to assess all Americans on all dimensions, and to use the information gained not just to place them in colleges and universities but to plot the whole course of their lives. That was his dream.

---

56 Ibid., pp. 88–89.
57 Ibid., p. 69.
58 Lemann, *The Big Test*, p. 68.

The only problem is, as we have shown in the first two chapters of this book, standardized tests themselves really measure little, if anything at all, and they are hardly designed to highlight the capable or more gifted individual, but rather to punish them. They are, at best, a kind of pseudo-scientific phrenology, and the businesses profiting from them are perpetrating a kind of government-protected racket and fraud. But one thing remains clear: Chauncey sought nothing less than total power over an individual's life and its course through his standardized tests. Such tests were intended, from the outset, as a means of social engineering and governance.

There are other lurkers on the fringes as well, and we have repeatedly encountered them in this story, for they form another part of the pattern in the advocacy behind Common Core: the foundations of billionaire busybodies.

"The Business Model" of Billionaire Busybodies
Foundations and the Educational Industrial Complex
Measuring the Measures and Measurers

"...periodically public scandals occur when investigation reveals that even elite students know very little."

—

JOHN TAYLOR GATTO[1]

"Method is the fleshpot of those who live in metaphysical deserts"

—

C.S. LEWIS

The assumptions of James Bryant Conant, Henry Chauncey, and the "edugarchy" were, on the face of it, simplistic, for in assuming that there was a "natural aristocracy" whose right and competency to rule was manifest in the accumulation of wealth and power could not, ultimately, be sustained by empirical observation. Indeed, one need only recall the case of the Rockefellers and Abraham Flexner's "Lincoln school," examined in the previous pages, to note the discomfort of one Rockefeller with an activity that epitomizes literacy and intelligence: reading.

To state it as succinctly as possible, there is no demonstrable logical relationship between wealth and power on the one hand, and intelligence on the other. Similarly, there is no demonstrable logical relationship between

---

[1] John Taylor Gatto, *Dumbing Us Down: The Hidden Curriculum of Compulsory Schooling* (Gabriola Island, British Columbia: New Society Publishers, 2005), pp. 17–18.

wealth and power, and the ability to rule competently and justly. The ability to drill oil, use "strongmen" to rough up the competition in order to create a railroad-oil-banking trust, the ability to create a mediocre computer operating system and to earn billions from it from its constant updates, the ability to build large steel mills, or casinos, or the ability to use "old school" connections to enter the "intelligence community" and parlay those connections into money and dubious covert operations, signify an intelligence and aptitude only for those things, not a general depth and breadth of culture, intelligence, spiritual virtue, or aptitude for the just uses of power and authority.

In advancing the exhibits in evidence for these propositions, one need only think of Hillary Clinton, John D. Rockefeller, Jeb Bush, Bernie Sanders, Donald Trump, or Bill Gates. If anything, the exhibits in evidence would suggest the opposite: that extremes of wealth, irrationality, narcissism and psychopathy seem to go hand in hand. Nor should this be taken as a rhetorical comment, for as will be seen in this chapter, the very wealthy have been driving the "dumbing down" agenda for a very long time, and for very specific reasons. Simply put, the billionaire busybodies behind the "edugarchy" are of mediocre intelligence and ability, and people of mediocre intelligence and ability can only be made to appear smarter and more capable than they really are by a commensurate dumbing-down of everyone else. All new riches eventually become "old money," and "old money" eventually becomes corrupt, seeking only its own preservation.

The policy is as old as oligarchy and plutocracy themselves, as John Taylor Gatto notes:

> In one of the strange ironies of history, Adam Smith's own publisher, William Playfair, chided Smith for his innocence. The social order to which he and Smith belonged was held together by deliberately depriving most people of information they needed to maximize opportunities. If secrets were promiscuously distributed, the ladders of privilege would collapse, their own children would be plunged back into the common stew. It was unthinkable. The familiar expression, "a little knowledge is a dangerous thing" was Playfair's invention. "Proper" schooling teaches "negatively," it never allows the working classes or the poor to read sufficiently well to understand what they do read."
>
> Set down clearly over 200 years ago, here is the recipe for the schools we commonly experience. Playfair argued that public instruction would ruin national prosperity, not enhance it... "The education of the middling and

lower ranks" has to be put aside, to be replaced with psychological conditioning in habits and attitudes of deference, envy, appetite, and mistrust of self, if the system of capitalism is to survive with all the benefits it provides.

"A smattering of learning is a very dangerous thing," he said, not because ordinary people are too dumb to learn; just the opposite, they are too smart to be allowed to learn.[2]

Reflecting back on previous chapters, this is exactly the pattern in evidence, for we have seen the entry of the notion of stimulus-response thinking, and its underlying materialist reduction of the human person, into American education whence it spread globally by dint of America's position of leadership in the post-World War II world. With this introduction, the need for constant "assessment" became a priority, since it was necessary to continually assess the effectiveness of various programs and approaches to this conditioning and its goal of the removal of the individual and his or her own responsibility and creativity.[3]

As was also seen, this activity was supported by foundation money, which allowed the families supporting them not only to launder their image and money by sponsoring "good works," but to do so while promoting their own private agendas.[4] With the introduction of foundation-sponsored stimulus-response educational philosophy and techniques, schools and pedagogy became psychologized, with a corresponding shift of focus from the content of specific disciplines, to a focus on method and social behavior itself, as schools became "compulsory behavior clinics":

Psychology currently constitutes the principal philosophical underpinning of our educational and, consequently, of our cultural outlook. From its largely bestial precepts major decisions in all walks of life are not made, and anyone attempting to determine the causes of a deep and lengthy national malaise must take into account psychology's covert hegemony over the tough processes of the body politic, the body economic, and the body social.

... This idea (that Man is a stimulus-response animal) and the methods it implies, has played a critical role in transforming The American Dream into a national nightmare.[5]

---

2   John Taylor Gatto, *Weapons of Mass Instruction*, pp. 106–107.
3   Paolo Lionni, *The Leipzig Connection*, pp. 39–40.
4   Ibid., pp. 49–50, 59, 62.
5   Ibid., pp. 88–89.

As we have also seen, this shift from the content of academic disciplines to the psychological focus was reflected in a similar restructuring of the disciplines themselves, with, for example, Dewey's abandonment of those disciplines in favor of an emphasis on the design of appropriate "activities" to socialize students, or to Abraham Flexner's abandonment of traditional academic subjects.[6]

Indeed, one can safely say that the entire American experiment with "progressive education" has been a disastrous flirtation with the gnostic techniques of cultural revolution writ large, since it was under the aegis "of improving teaching *methods*" that a wholesale revolution in "*what* was taught" was effected.[7] For example, history, geography, sociology, economics, political science, and so on, were all thrown into a pot, stirred, and served up as a stew of disconnected factoids called "social studies."[8]

But with the advent of the Internet, the computer, and digital databases, the idea of individualized "assessment" which is at the heart of Common Core, and the psychological turn in schooling, has been given a new emphasis and a heightened degree of precision and control that the progressivist educational theorists of yesteryear could only dream of.

Our focus in the remainder of this chapter, then, is on the historical development of this technological focus, and on the large money foundations behind it, the pattern of their operation, and the implications for the assessment process of Common Core.

A. The Technology Factor and the Education-Industrial Complex:
1. The Computer, Standardized Tests, and Operant Conditioning of the Student

In 1992 a prophetic book of great relevance to the issue of the Common Core adaptive assessment process was published by Lewis Perelman, titled *School's Out: Hyperlearning, the New Technology, and the End of Education*. The book

---

6   Paolo Lionni, *The Leipzig Connection*, p. 72.

7   John A. Stormer, *None Dare Call It Treason* (Florissant, MO: Liberty Bell Press, 1964), p. 99.

8   Ibid., p. 105. Stormer, like many others, points to the fact that this stew was the recommended recipe of yet another in the Wundtian succession, Dr. Harold Rugg, in a seventeen-volume study Conclusions and Recommendations of the American Historical Association for the teaching of "social studies," a study overseen by radical progressivist educator George S. Counts (q.v. p. 105).

was the product of Perelman's having been a senior research fellow of the Hudson Institute for three years, an association which inexorably ties him, and his book, to the Hudson Institute's major funders: the conservative Koch Family Foundation, Castle Rock Foundation, the John M. Olin Foundation, the Lynde and Harry Bradley Foundation, and the Scaife Foundation.[9] In his books, Perelman reflected the ideological commitment of the hidden foundation money backing the Hudson Institute, for he maintained that human teachers were becoming obsolescent if not obsolete, since teaching could be performed much more efficiently by technology.

> He called for a major overhaul of the nation's schools that would transform teaching from the traditional, human-intensive activity we know into a machine-intensive one. He claimed that teachers could be replaced by computers and the only reason this had not yet occurred was that the academic establishment and the "educrats" were not allowing it to happen.[10]

This move toward the mechanization of education implies the redefinition of teachers from their conventional role to being merely "facilitators" ensuring the efficiency of the student-computer interface.

With this, one is once again chin-to-chin with the stimulus-response psychology that has been driving educational methodology since the progressives infiltrated and co-opted American schooling. Behavioral psychologist B.F. Skinner's "Skinner box" or Pavlov's ringing bells and salivating dogs could now be engineered to a whole range of stimulus-response mechanisms appropriate to humans, employing the growing possibilities of ever-expanding computer technology based upon programmed instruction and responses,[11] as exemplified in standardized tests.

While this may seem to epitomize the inherent problems and philosophy behind the adaptive assessment process of Common Core, the roots and possibilities of the technology were foreseen in a 1963 publication of the National Educational Association, published under a contract with the U.S. Department of Health, Education, and Welfare. The publication, *The Role of the Computer in Future Instructional Systems*, contained a chapter titled

---

9   Anthony G. Picciano and Joel Spring, *The Great American Education-Industrial Complex: Ideology, Technology, and Profit*, pp. 56–57.

10 Ibid., p. 42.

11 Anthony G. Picciano and Joel Spring, *The Great American Educational-Industrial Complex: Ideology, Technology, and Profit*, p. 43.

"Effortless Learning, Attitude Changing, and Training in Decision-Making" in which one encounters the first adumbrations of the adaptive assessment process of Common Core, and the psychological underpinnings behind it:

> Another area of potential development in computer applications is *the atti-tude-changing machine*. Dr. Bertram Raven in the Psychology Department at the University of California at Los Angeles is in the process of building *a computer-based device for changing attitudes*. This device will work on the principle that students' attitudes can be changed effectively by using the Soc-ratic method of asking an appropriate series of leading questions designed to right the balance between appropriate attitudes, and those deemed less acceptable. For instance, after first determining a student's constellation of attitudes through appropriate testing procedures, the machine would calculate which attitudes are "out of phase" and which of these are amenable to change. If the student were opposed to foreign trade, say, and a favorable disposition were sought for, *the machine would select an appropriate series of statements and questions organized to right the imbalance in the student's attitudes*. The machine, for instance, would have detected that the student liked President Kennedy and was against the spread of Communism; there-fore, the student would be shown that JFK favored foreign trade and that foreign trade to underdeveloped countries helped to arrest the Communist infiltration of these governments.[12]

Of course, the Socratic method is being deliberately perverted here, for in its original form, the asking of leading questions was designed to elicit discovery and knowledge, not to "adjust" or change attitudes. And needless to say, who is to determine which attitudes are appropriate? Once one admits that an individual's attitudes can be "adjusted" by an adaptive computerized process, the need for constant monitoring of that individual throughout their entire "school life" becomes a requirement to the system, until, as an adult, an individual's attitudes have been "adjusted" and "frozen."

---

12 National Education Association, *The Role of the Computer in Future Instruc-tional Systems*, March/April 1963 supplement, Audiovisual Communication Review, Monograph 2, Technological Development Project of the National Educational Association (Contract #SAE9073, U.S. Office of Education, Department of Health, Education, and Welfare: Washington, DC, 1963), cited in Charlotte Thomson Iserbyt, *The Deliberate Dumbing Down of America*, p. 85, emphases added.

We submit that this paper and those like it are the real philosophical and technological beginnings of the Common Core assessment process, for note that one is now faced not only with Banesh Hoffmann's criticism that the student must read the mind of some remote and anonymous committee of test-preparing experts on the *content* of questions of standardized tests, but also read the minds *and value systems* of those same anonymous committees and their psychological, metaphysical, and moral assumptions.

It takes little imagination to see how such a process would be beneficial to global corporations as a mechanism for "adjusting the attitudes" of those opposed to their policies. One can easily imagine, for example, a series of "leading questions" designed to elicit favorable responses to "free trade" or collective activities and responsibilities, and few, if any, questions on the merits of protective tariffs or individual rights and freedoms.

What was a dream in 1963 became a reality in 1971, as the University of Pittsburgh's Learning Research and Development Center created "the Individually Prescribed Instruction model"[13] in 1963, and followed this with experimental field testing, the results of which were published in 1971:

> Out of this experience grew the current Individually Prescribed Instruction project in which various combinations of instructional materials, testing procedures, and teacher practices are being used to accommodate individual student differences.
>
> IPI is a system based on a set of specified objectives correlated with diagnostic instruments, curriculum materials, teaching techniques, and management capabilities. The objectives of the system are:
>
> 1. to permit student mastery of instructional content at individual learning rates;
> 2. to ensure active student involvement in the learning process;
> 3. to encourage student involvement in learning through self-directed and self-initiated activities;
> 4. to encourage evaluation of progress toward mastery and to provide instructional materials and techniques based on individual needs and styles.[14]

---

13   Charlotte Thomson Iserbyt, op. cit., p. 85.
14   David S. Bushnell, ed., *Planned Change in Education: A Systems Approach* (New York: Harcourt, Brace, and Jovanovich, 1971), p. 95, cited in Charlotte Thomson Iserbyt, *The Deliberate Dumbing Down of America*, p. 86.

If all this sounds like a perfectly wonderful return to the one-room schoolhouse and its mingling of different ages of children all being taught, at different rates of individual learning, by the overworked and underpaid teacher, think again, for remember that the goal is ultimately to replace the teacher with the computer and an individually adapted constant assessment process. One may think of the experiment as a trial run of Common Core in this respect. On this view, and on the wider view of the stimulus-response individually adaptive computerized assessment process, the student is "input," and the school "which modifies his capabilities toward certain goals and objectives" is "output."[15] The student is the hardware, and the assessment process is the software.

It is important to understand that behind the language of "mastery learning" lurks the Wundtian technique of stimulus-response and Skinnerian "operant conditioning,"[16] and in this, one recognizes a further "gnostic tactic" of the edugarchs, namely, that of disguising revolutionary goals and/or techniques behind euphemistic terminology. Indeed, as Charlotte Thomson Iserbyt, a former Reagan Administration Department of Education appointee, observes, the entire method of operation of the modern American government, not to mention its school system and indeed its general culture, operates through such stimulus-response and operant conditioning techniques: "Those individuals and agencies conforming with government policies, criteria, etc., are rewarded, whereas those who do not conform are either ignored or denied special privileges and funding."[17] As one observer of this trend remarked, "local change agents are able to facilitate a group to a consensus in support of predetermined goals by using familiar, traditional terms which carry the new behaviorist meanings."[18] The meaning of "teacher" is thus "facilitator" or "change agent," and the meaning of "mastery learning" is "operant conditioning."

Yet another "trial run" laying the foundations for the Common Core adaptive assessment process was conducted in Hawaii in 1969, whose state

---

15 *Learning and Instruction* (Chicago Inner City Schools Position Paper, June 1968), cited in Charlotte Thomson Iserbyt, *The Deliberate Dumbing Down of America*, p. 97. Thomson Iserbyt also notes that this paper referenced Soviet Preschool Education, translated by none other than Educational Testing Service's edugarch Henry Chauncey!

16 Charlotte Thomson Iserbyt, *The Deliberate Dumbing Down of America*, p. 99.

17 Ibid., p. 100.

18 Ibid., pp. 127–128. The speaker in question was Mary Thompson in 1972, a member of the California Republican Women's Federation.

Department of Education published its *Master Plan for Public Education in Hawaii—Toward a New Era for Education in Hawaii,* in which the basic philosophy of the Common Core assessment process was again prophetically stated, for "the computer," it says, "will enhance learning.... *The teacher will operate as a manager....* The teacher will have a ready record of each student's performance and a ready access to the information the student needs during each stage of his progress."[19] In this document, one also encounters another favorite meme of progressive education theorists:

> The task of the schools during the past stable, relatively unchanging world was to emphasize fixed habits, memorization of facts, and development of specific skills to meet known needs. But for a future which will include vast changes, the emphasis should be on how to meet new situations, on the skills of research, observation, analysis, logic and communication, on the development of attitudes appropriate to change, and on a commitment to flexibility and reason.
>
> Behavioral sciences subject matter should form a part of our modern curriculum to provide a basis for self-knowledge and behavioral concepts.... Study of ethical traditions, concepts and changes in value structure should be emphasized.... Department of Education [sic] should experiment with the group therapy, role playing and encounter group approach that are professionally planned and conducted, as a basis for understanding other people, races, cultures, and points of view.[20]

We would respectfully submit that in a rapidly changing and unstable world that the stability provided by traditional education with its emphasis on content, facts, analysis, and grounding in basic history are essential to providing not only a basis of stability, but the very basis for the analysis, logic, communication called for by the paper. Or to put it differently, the world is *always* changing, and there is no logical connection between change in the world and the need to abandon content-driven academic disciplines for the psychological and sociological focus of which modern educational theorists are so enamored. Indeed, we've been hearing about this need for change from the professional educators for over a century, and yet they have produced a

---

19 Department of Education, State of Hawaii, *Master Plan for Education in Hawaii— Toward a New Era for Education in Hawaii,* p. 36, cited in Thomson Iserbyt, *The Deliberate Dumbing Down of America,* p. 104.

20 Ibid., pp. 50–52, cited in Thomson Iserbyt, op. cit. p. 105.

population which, due to its increasing ignorance and barbarism, is even *less* capable of evaluating change critically than its ancestors.

These attitudes are summarized by Leonard S. Kenworthy in an astonishingly honest set of statements made to an international conference of fellow "educators":

> Here and there teachers have modified individual courses.... Schools have rewritten syllabi or added courses.... But nowhere has there been a rigorous examination of the total experiences of children and/or youth in schools and *the development of a continuous, cumulative, comprehensive curriculum to create the new type of people needed for effective living in the latter part of the 20ᵗʰ century....*
>
> *...All the work we do in developing internationally minded individuals should be directed toward improved behavior.*
>
> That means that all the efforts in this dimension of education must be predicated on *the research in the formation, reinforcement, and change of attitudes and on the development of skills. Knowledge is tremendously important, but we should be clear by now that it must be carefully selected knowledge, discovered by the learners rather than told to them, and organized by them with the help of teachers or professors around concepts*, generalizations, or big ideas. Teaching, therefore, becomes the process of helping younger people to probe, discover, analyze, compare, and contrast rather than telling.
>
> ...
>
> *Changed behavior is our goal and it consists in large measure of improved attitudes, improved skills, and carefully selected knowledge*—these three—and the greatest of these is attitudes...[21]

Indeed, it never seems to occur to the theorists that in a world of change, some *fixity* and tradition, some *knowledge* in breadth and in depth, rather than vague and platitudinous focus on "skills" and "attitudes" might be a *good* thing.

---

21   Leonard S. Kenworthy, "The International Dimension of Education: Background Paper II Prepared for the World Conference on Education," Asilomar, California, March 4–15, 1970, pp. 23–39, cited in Thomson Iserbyt, *The Deliberate Dumbing Down of America*, pp. 116–117, emphases added.

2. Teacher Evaluation as Operant Conditioning

If standardized tests are operant conditioning of students, then an *adaptive* testing process coordinated by computers and remote, anonymous programmers with unknown cosmological assumptions, one following the individual student from their entry into and exit from the school system, will be operant conditioning on steroids, a kind of sorting mechanism that Henry Chauncey and James Bryant Conant could only dream of.

But if standardized testing is an operant conditioning of students, then what is it for teachers if not the same thing? After all, they are the ones being asked to function as the human extension of the computer in administering the tests, and more importantly, they are the ones who must "teach to the test." This very fact points out yet another effect of the whole "cosmology of the global Skinner Box" that American education has become. Recall that Dr. Banesh Hoffmann's critique of the standardized test was that it more often than not punished "the finer mind"; students were not required to *generate* answers and then articulate them; they were merely required to *select* from a pre-selected list[22] prepared by "experts" whose qualifications, as Hoffmann showed, were not only anonymous but dubious. For the teacher "teaching to the test," this results in a kind of operant conditioning of its own, because the teacher must "dumb down" his or her presentation of the subject, *particularly* with respect to the more gifted student.

The result is a homogenization of pedagogical styles, a homogenization even of the *personae* of teachers, and this, too, is an *explicit goal*, for Charlotte Thomson Iserbyt cites an article that appeared in the *Newport Harbor Ensign* of Corona del Mar, California, in January 1972, following the passage of yet another "education" bill in the state legislature. The article notes that "A teacher will no longer have the prerogative of having his own 'style' of teaching, because he will be held 'accountable' to *uniform expected student progress. His job will **depend** on how well he can produce 'intended' behavioral changes in students.*"[23] While Common Core with its *individually adaptive* assessment process might seem far removed from this "uniformity" approach, the truth is, to a certain extent, the opposite, for individual adaptability implies the presence of *hidden personality type*

---

22 Alfie Kohn, *The Case Against Standardized Testing: Raising the Scores, Ruining the Schools* (Portsmouth, NH: Heinemann, 2000), p. 11.

23 Charlotte Thomson Iserbyt, *The Deliberate Dumbing Down of America*, p. 124, all emphases added.

testing within the assessment process, and a statistical approach to the individual. The teacher, in short, will not only have to "teach to a test" which is standardized, as in the old form of test, but now also have to teach to a test which is supposedly adapting to each individual student, multiplying the ambiguity in the system.

The article in the *Newport Harbor Ensign*, however, goes on to disclose that the teachers themselves had to acquire the "skills" necessary to perform their new tasks, and here is where, once again, "continuing education" at the hands of our dreaded facilitator Robert/a comes in:

> FORMAL TRAINING SESSIONS: participants attended two 2 1/2-hour sessions to acquire the prerequisite tools. Evidence was collected to show that by the end of the final training session, 80% of the participants had acquired a minimal level of ability to apply these competencies.
> PREREQUISITE TOOLS: Teachers learning how to identify or diagnose strengths and weaknesses, learning to write and use behavioral objectives, learning new teaching techniques and procedures, etc. [sic][24] Teachers learn these through workshops and in-service training, having acquired these skills, teachers had to go through the "appraisal" technique.[25]

That this is operant conditioning is revealed by one very obvious fact, one moreover that the reader is encountering over and over: the mandated-attendance "continuing education" workshops that teachers attend *are seldom, if ever, related to the latest scholarship or research in the disciplines they teach—art, literature, biology, mathematics, physics, and so on—but are really about socialization games (usually of a passive-aggressive nature) designed firstly to ensure the teacher remains "on the reservation," and secondly are equipped to be the behavior modifier, the change agent, that the system requires.*

This rather obvious though often unremarked-upon point, we suggest, is the strongest evidence—the proof staring us in the face, so to speak—that the whole apparatus of modern American education, from its colleges of "education" to its teacher certification, to its standardized, and now individually adapted computerized, assessments are not about imparting the academic contents of disciplines, nor about logic, reason, morality, or the inculcation of individual virtue and responsibility. It is really about *socialization* and

---

24 Note the lack of a grammatical sentence.
25 Ibid., pp. 124–125.

about *method*, and the continual assessment of teacher and student that the passive-aggressive techniques of socialization are "taking hold."

If we seem to be belaboring this point, it is because it is an important one, a point that can be appreciated by asking a simple question: If you are a teacher who happens to be reading this book, ask yourself when the last time was that your school district paid for you to attend any conference about the *subject* matter of the discipline you teach. Note we said *the subject matter*, and *not* new methods of teaching it, nor the latest state or federal requirements in the field, but *the subject matter itself*. When was the last time your school district, or principal, paid your way to a conference where the latest papers in mathematics, biology, literary criticism, philosophy, were read and discussed? And if you were able to answer that question, then another occurs: when was the last time you were required to attend such conferences? Do the requirements to attend continuing education events in the subject matter of your discipline equal the number of times you were required to attend events concerning the latest *methodological theory or behavior modification event?*

One gains an historical appreciation that American education is *not* about the transmission of the traditions of those disciplines, but about behavior modification, from the fact that from 1973 to 1975, the U.S. Department of Education has helped to fund the publication of Ronald G. Havelock's *The Change Agent's Guide to Innovation in Education*, published by Educational Technology Publishing of Englewood Cliffs, New Jersey.[26] The title says it all, and prompts the question "Why is it that the change agents' plans and their tools to 'transform' our educational system never change, while parents and teachers are told, repeatedly, that they must be ready and willing to change?"[27]

3. Schools as Change Agents: Social Engineering, "Lifetime Learning Accounts," and the Harvesting of the Individual

The answer to that question should, by now, be evident: perpetual change empowers the edugarchy and the "testing industry," but perpetual change can only occur in the atmosphere of perpetual failure, which creates the need for ever more refined methods of socialization disguised as pedagogical "method." The final goal was indeed an *individually adaptive* process—such

---

26 Charlotte Thomson Iserbyt, *The Deliberate Dumbing Down of America*, p. 137.
27 Ibid.

as the individually adaptive assessment process of Common Core—as the following statements of Lawrence P. Grayson, made in 1976, suggest:

> Behavioral science, which is assuming an increasing role in educational technology, promises to make educational techniques more effective by recognizing individual differences among students and *by patterning instruction to meet individual needs*. However, behavioral science is more than an unbiased means to an end. It has a basic value position based on the premise that such 'values as freedom and democracy, which imply that the individual ultimately has free will and is responsible for his own actions, are not only cultural inventions, but illusions.' This position is contradictory to the basic premise of freedom and is demeaning to the dignity of the individual.[28]

The idea of individually adaptive instruction (and hence, the inevitable individually adaptive assessment that comes with it) becomes the mechanism driving the need for perpetual "continuing education" on an *individual basis*, leading one educational theorist, Luvern L. Cunningham, to propose in 1980 that each American citizen have a "lifetime learning account."[29] We strongly suspect that if ever implemented, the credits of that account would probably be designed to pay for the type of "facilitator workshops" that teachers must endure, rather than be spent on actual books on actual subjects. Such a method would fit the time-honored method of oligarchies everywhere by making people pay for the very methods and products that enslave them.

We have suggested thus far that one of the principal goals of such outcome-based "education" is to inculcate the mentality of the "global Skinner box," a mentality deliberately designed to sever both student and teacher from the tradition or history of the very disciplines they ostensibly are to teach or learn. A deliberate goal—though one often left carefully and guardedly unstated—is to change individual and group social memory itself, to rewrite history. As much as this was admitted by Benjamin Bloom, the so-called "'father' of the Effective Schools Research method," who insisted that education's purpose was to "change the thoughts, feelings, and actions of students."[30] Yet another advocate of this approach was Thomas A. Kelly, who insisted that the brain—presumably the brains of teachers

---

28 Lawrence P. Grayson, "Education, Technology, and Individual Privacy," ECTJ,
     Vol. 28, No. 3, 1976, 195–208, cited in Charlotte Thomson Iserbyt, op. cit., p. 152.
29 Charlotte Thomson Iserbyt, *The Deliberate Dumbing Down of America*, p. 181.
30 Ibid., p. 176.

and students—should not be used for storage, i.e., *content*, but for process-ing.[31] With an individually adaptive computer assessment process such as is being advocated for Common Core, a process to follow students *as individuals* (and their teachers!) throughout their educational life, the ability to "fine-tune" responses to hidden agendas for the collective, eventually to be expanded to a global scale as we have seen, increases exponentially. Coupled with the emergence of the "electronic textbook" with all its implicit dangers of texts able to be modified or "appropriately adjusted" at the touch of a button, and the dangerous implication arises that history itself, that human memory itself, could be altered or engineered.[32]

B. The Foundations Factor:
1. Tests, "Deschooling," and Governance

All of the preceding nonsense could not have been inflicted on our teachers and students without a lot of money driving it, and we have repeatedly pointed out in the preceding chapters the influence of the foundations of the very wealthy not only in funding the schemes of the edugarchs, but in funding their advocacy. The consistent role—one is inclined to say culpability—of these foundations throughout the story has contributed in no small measure to the rise of the interlocked system of special interests, the teachers' colleges, the departments of education within academia and government, the endless "continuing edu-cation workshops," that has led Anthony G. Picciano and Joel Spring to call the phenomenon, with a great deal of insight and profundity, the "education-al-industrial complex." This phenomenon is defined by its complex of goals, motivations, and networked connections and alliances, in order to promote (1) the goal of the expanded role of technology in the classroom throughout the entire public education system, from kindergarten through the final year of high school, (2) the shrinking role of the teachers and parents, (3) the removal of state and local oversight and accountability and its replacement by corporate and bureaucratic regulatory bodies unaccountable to the public or its institutions of

---

31   Ibid.

32   Charlotte Thomson Iserbyt, *The Deliberate Dumbing Down of America*, p. 185: Thomson Iserbyt cites Professor Benjamin Bloom once again, in a work pub-lished in 1981, *All Our Children Learning*, on the need for the adoption of interna-tional standards for curricula, tests, and so on, to be reached by "consensus" of international experts.

government, and finally (4) their continued profits by the creation of a privileged system of alliances designed to promote their technologies and administrative services in promotion of their own ideologies.[33]

The mechanism for "accountability" in such a system is as it has been all along: the standardized computerized test, which in the ideology of the business-oriented neo-conservative and conservative right in more recent times was almost exactly the same ideology of the progressivist left of the turn of the last century, for the ideology at work was that of materialism, mechanism, and consumerism. Schools, so the new mantra goes, should be accountable like a business, with the "balance sheet" reflecting the measures of constant testing and assessment, a formula reducing teachers, students, and families to the status of consumers of a product (one, notably, to which to *real* competition exists and one which is given standard mercantilist government protection and promotion).[34] It is no accident, therefore, that at recent *New York Times* educational conferences no teachers were invited, while the rostrum of speakers included 29 corporate representatives in a total list of 37 speakers.[35] It is no accident that these corporate sponsors promote "virtual schools"[36] with electronic textbooks—amendable, remember, at the touch of a button—or that the No Child Left Behind Act specifically mentioned the role of corporations in analyzing testing data.[37]

Nowhere is this intersection of the educational-industrial complex's interests and those of the professional edugarchy more in evidence than in the advocacy for Common Core,[38] for Common Core is *not* about the idea of having a standard of content. This issue is, in our opinion, a non-starter, for *every* academic discipline, from theology to law, has a standard by which its academic study is measured. The problem with Common Core, once again, is the *assessment process* behind it, and the further empowerment of un-accountable "experts" designing its adaptive assessment process. The goal of "privatizing" education has as one consequence the ability to short-circuit any real public discussion, debate, or control over

---

33 Anthony G. Picciano and Joel Spring, *The Great American Educational-Industrial Complex: Ideology, Technology, and Profit*, p. 2.
34 Anthony G. Picciano and Joel Spring, *The Great American Educational-Industrial Complex*, pp. 4–5.
35 Ibid., p. 7.
36 Ibid., p. 6.
37 Ibid., p. 18.
38 Ibid., p. 17.

the process.[39] A key factor in this removal of the voter—including teachers—from the debate has been the creation of the unelected task force of experts, who then make their recommendations to state and federal government agencies.[40] We have seen thus far that one goal of the eugarchs and their foundation backers has been to transform the teaching profession itself into a "change agent," and even to dramatically reduce the role of the teacher in the classroom. From the "business standpoint" of some of Common Core's backers, this amounts to nothing less than union busting.[41] In such an educational universe, in the cosmology of the Global Skinner Box, "testing efficiency" and improved scores equal productivity.[42]

The goal of significantly reducing the role of the teacher, or even of eliminating it altogether, a goal that one paper calls "deschooling,"[43] is all a component of a wider pattern of eliminating popular government and voter oversight in the name of "privatization," which, with the removal of the teacher, and the "outsourcing" of their function to remote "experts" planning the questions on tests, results in a new system of governance, since the effect on existing public institutions is to create "Swiss-cheese governments lacking sufficient regulators to oversee privatized government services."[44] Again, this is a classic case of union busting, dressed up in clever euphemisms.

We, your authors, are acutely aware that there is historical evidence to suggest that the hierarchies of the teachers' unions were radicalized almost from their inception. However, we would also suggest that in the contempo-

---

39 Picciano and Spring, op. cit., p. 29. Picciano and Spring point out that the Gates Foundation targets change in specific state laws, often for the purpose of making online education more palatable to local communities.

40 Charlotte Thomson Iserbyt, *The Deliberate Dumbing Down of America*, p. 190.

41 Picciano and Spring, op. cit., pp. 22–23. Picciano and Spring point out that one recent goal of the edugarchs, given the attempt to increase the role of technology, is the removal of the cap on the amount of students per classroom. (p. 23): "Proposals to expand online instruction and, as a result, reduce the cost of teachers' salaries, are presented as answers to declining state education budgets." They also point out that the recent economic crises were viewed as crises of opportunity in order to accomplish this goal. Picciano and Spring also point out the crucial fact that the Foundation for Excellence in education is headed by Jeb Bush, and receives significant funding from the Gates Foundation.

42 Ibid., p. 38: Picciano and Spring make the insightful observation that "education unlike other endeavors, has always been characterized as a high-touch human activity based largely on teacher-student relationships that extend over time. It has rarely been characterized as an automated production of goods or services."

43 Ibid., p. 39.

44 Picciano and Spring, op. cit., p. 38.

rary situation, they may be the last thing connecting the public to any real possibility of oversight of their children's education. In that respect, we would have you consider the history of:

2. The Power and Unaccountability of Foundations

Consider, for a moment, the following hypothetical: imagine you have made several billion dollars drilling for and discovering oil, and, to ensure your position, you've hired a few thugs to crack the skulls of your opposition together, bought a railroad, undercut the competition's transport costs, bought a bank, and in general, gained a dubious reputation in spite of all the good you claim to have done. You hire a public relations expert, who tells you it's all a matter of perception, and that you simply have to change the public's perception of you. Thus advised, you cleverly arrange for photographers to be present when you hand out dimes and lollipops to young children in a kindly, grandfatherly way. Additionally, wanting to protect your billions of dollars from the taxman, you also use your wealth and power to create a federal law by buying a few corrupt politicians.[45] They create a law whereby one can donate all of one's wealth to a philanthropic foundation, where, because it is ostensibly serving the public good—or at least pretending to do so behind the bland and reassuring euphemisms of its corporate charter—it remains tax-free, and can be used to promote all sorts of cultural and political agendas.

The scheme, and scam, is a brilliant one, for it allows the super-rich to achieve through the *control* what they could not achieve through the *ownership* of their own wealth, for now, tax-free, it is allowed to grow and grow in escrow accounts, and to be used to extend private agendas, all with government exemptions and protections. This gives the "philanthropic" foundations a measure of power and influence exceeding that even of banks and insurance companies. They are unique public actors, in that while their activities are often designed to drive and mold public opinion, institutions and culture, they themselves are almost totally unaccountable to any institution of government at any level, local, state, or federal.

Not surprisingly, these entities became a focus of federal congressional

---

45   We realize, unless proven otherwise by a preponderance of evidence, that the
     phrase "corrupt politicians" is a redundancy, corruption being a natural attribute
     of the species.

investigations after the end of World War II, during that era when a variety of congressional committees investigated this or that element of subversion within the body politic and broader culture. We tend to think of this era as the "McCarthy" era because of the Wisconsin senator's investigations of Communism in his Senate Government Operations Committee. But there were a number of other congressional investigations during this same crucial period of American history, in both houses, and sponsored by both political parties, into various areas of security breaches and suspected subversion, from the Mafia investigations of the Kefauver Committee, through the McCarthy Committee investigations of Communism, to the House Un-American Activities Committee investigations of the same issue, up to and including, of course, the house investigative committees on foundations, the Cox and Reece Committees. While an adequate integrated history of this period and its various committees has yet to be written in our opinion, the role of foundation advocacy for the educational system we have been examining in previous pages, and its advocacy for a wider cosmological and political agenda, compels a closer look at the postwar committees investigating them, and what they uncovered: the short-lived and stonewalled Cox Committee, and its successor, the Reece Committee, in the U.S. House of Representatives.

a. The Short-Lived Cox Committee, and Its Findings

The Cox Committee, named for its chairman, Congressman E.E. Cox, a Democrat of Georgia, was formed by a resolution of the U.S. House of Representatives on March 10, 1952, by a vote of 194 (100 Democrats, 94 Republicans) to 158 (88 Democrats, 69 Republicans, 1 Independent).[46] The committee that resulted was composed of four Democrats, including Cox himself, and three Republicans, including Congressman B. Carroll Reece from Tennessee,[47] whose Reece Committee would continue the investigation that the Cox Committee had begun.

---

46 René A. Wormser, *Foundations: The Power and Influence* (New York: Devin-Adair, 1958), p. 329.

47 Ibid., p. 330. Two of the majority Democratic members, Donald O'Toole of New York, and Alme J. Forand of Rhode Island, did not. The other Democrat members of the Cox Committee were Cox himself, and Brooks Hays of Arkansas. The Republican members, besides B. Carroll Reece, were Richard Simpson of Pennsylvania, and Angier Goodwin of Massachusetts.

The committee, during its short existence from March 1952 until the issuance of its final report in January 1953, struggled with a low budget, lack of an adequate investigation staff, and from significant opposition to its investigations from non-committee members from both parties. Nonetheless, in that final report, the Committee had concluded something profoundly disturbing:

> There can be no reasonable doubt concerning the efforts of the Communist Party both to infiltrate the foundations and to make use, so far as it was possible, of foundation grants to finance Communist causes and Communist sympathizers. The committee is satisfied that as long as 20 years ago Moscow decided upon a program *of infiltrating cultural and educational groups and organizations in this country including the foundations.*[48]

In support of these assertions, the Cox Committee pointed to the "ugly unalterable fact" that Alger Hiss had been president of one such large foundation, the Carnegie Endowment for International Peace.[49] Additionally, it briefly mentioned the role of the Carnegie Corporation, the Carnegie Endowment for International Peace, and the Rockefeller Foundation in funding the notorious Institute for Pacific Relations,[50] which had been under constant fire in the postwar era from other committees such as the McCarran and McCarthy committees, for the role of many of its most famous members in the fall of Chiang Kai-Shek's Nationalist China, and the beginning of Communist China.

At the end of the Cox Committee's short duration, minority member Carroll Reece of Tennessee appended an endorsement of his own, pointing out the committee's inadequate budget and short duration, calling for a new committee to continue its work. After the Republican congressional sweep of 1952, the Reece Committee was passed by House resolution and given until January 1955 to complete its work.[51]

---

48 Final Report of the Cox Committee, January 1, 1953, No 2514, 82nd Congress, 2nds Session, cited in Wormser, op. cit., p. 331, emphasis added.

49 René A. Wormser, *Foundations: Their Power and Influence*, p. 332.

50 Ibid., op. cit., pp. 332–333.

51 Ibid., pp. 335–337.

b. The Reece Committee Enabling Resolution

The Reece Committee found something very different than the pattern of "Communist subversion" alluded to by the Cox Committee, or rather, it discovered something very complementary to it. This, in part, was due to the somewhat more comprehensive brief it had been given in its enabling resolution:

> The committee is authorized and *directed* to conduct a full and complete investigation and study of educational and philanthropic foundations and other comparable organizations which are exempt from Federal income taxation *to determine if any foundations and organizations are using their resources for purposes other than the purposes for which they were established,* and especially to determine which such foundations and organizations are using their resources *for un-American and subversive activities; for political purposes; propaganda, or attempts to influence legislation.*[52]

The scope of this resolution meant that the findings of the Reece Committee were inevitably broader than those of its predecessor, and thus also inevitably much more thought-provoking.

We may group these findings into two broad categories: (1) substantive findings, dealing with the goals, ideological trends, and implicit philosophical assumptions of the foundations, and (2) methodological findings, dealing with the precise operational tactics by which their substantive goals were achieved.

3. The Reece Committee Findings
a. The Historical Parallels and Medieval Foundations

The principal problem of Foundations was, and remains, their nearly complete and total non-accountability to the public nor even to the states or federal government chartering them. In his testimony before the Reece Committee, Cornell University President Schurman, a trustee of the Carnegie Foundation, put the case for the Foundations' nearly limitless freedom of action. The Reece Committee's council, René Wormser, notes that

---

52   Ibid., p. 337, emphasis added by Wormser.

Among the permitted foundation activities he listed: defense of the
Republic in times of war; economic and political reforms which the
trustees deem essential to the vitality and efficiency of the Republic in
time of peace; championship for free trade or protectionism; advocacy
of socialism or individualism; underwriting the respective programs of
the Republican or Democratic parties; introduction of Buddhism in the
United States.[53]

As such, the Foundations effectively become not only tax-free havens for
the wealth of the very rich, they become a means for those families to retain
the control of that wealth, and to direct the use of that power to direct and
mold public opinion and government policy. They remain enormous con-
centrations of power in private hands, granted by government charters.[54]
"In this manner," writes Reece Committee counsel Wormser, "and by other
uses of foundations, control of an enterprise is often retained by a family,
while a huge part of a decedent's fortune is removed from death taxes."[55]
They are thus "instruments for the retention of control over capital assets
that would otherwise be lost";[56] in other words, they are instruments for the
inter-generational accumulation of capital, and the very basis on which a
dynasty of capital functions.

If this is beginning to sound a bit familiar, that's because it is, for even the
Reece Committee's counsel Wormser pointed out its obvious resemblance
to the medieval military crusading order of the Knights Templar, who, like
the foundations of today, were exempt from local and national taxation laws,
whose members (or, to use today's Foundation terms, "trustees") held no
equity position in the Order, but who nonetheless wielded great financial
power, since the Order *itself* could accumulate inter-generational wealth and
property. And, like the Foundations of today, the Templars were engaged in
political activity, an activity that, in their attempt to found their own Templar
state, was ultimately subversive to the very institution that had chartered
their existence, the papacy.[57] In some cases, the modern foundations even
more closely resemble those of their Renaissance counterparts in the Italian
city-states, where corporations of the oligarchs in turn created other corpora-

---

53 René A. Wormser, *Foundations: Their Power and Influence*, p. 12.
54 Ibid., p.5.
55 René A. Wormser, *Foundations: Their Power and Influence*, p. xi.
56 Ibid., p. x.
57 Ibid., p. 17.

tions to manage the oligarchs' money; in effect, the foundations of today as "juridical persons created by juridical persons,"[58] behind which hide the real persons of the families controlling their wealth.

The modern foundations, like the medieval crusading orders, were chartered oligarchies without real oversight or public accountability:

> These dangers relate chiefly to the use of foundation funds for political ends; they arise out of the accumulation of substantial economic power and of cultural influence in the hands of a class of administrators of tax-exempt funds established in perpetuity. An "elite" has thus emerged, in control of gigantic financial resources operating outside of our democratic processes, which is willing and able to shape the future of this nation and of mankind in the image of its own value concepts. An unparalleled amount of power is concentrated increasingly in the hands of an interlocking and self-per- petuating group. *Unlike the power of corporate management, it is unchecked by stockholders; unlike the power of government, it is unchecked by the people; unlike the power of churches, it is unchecked by any firmly established canons of value.*[59]

This means something else, equally significant, for just as a foundation is a means for the very wealthy to retain *control* over their wealth without retaining *ownership* of it, and hence, allows them to use it to retain, main- tain, and expand their control over society and its activities, this means that foundation activity or advocacy of a certain policy implies the personal or familial advocacy of that policy, and their desire to use it as a basis for the maintenance and/or expansion of their power. As we have seen in previous chapters, this is precisely the pattern in evidence from foundation support for early progressive education projects, a fact that was not lost upon the Reece Committee, nor on its counsel René Wormser:

> A very powerful complex of foundations and allied organizations has devel- oped over the years to exercise a high degree of control over education. Part of this complex, and ultimately responsible for it, are the Rockefeller and Carnegie groups of foundations. The largest of the foundation giants, The Ford Foundation, is a late comer. It has now joined in the complex and its

---

58 Ibid., p. 55.

59 René A. Wormser, *Foundations: Their Power and Influence*, pp. vii–viii, emphasis added.

impact is tremendous; but the operations of the Carnegie and Rockefeller groups start way back.[60]

Of course, the situation has changed since Wormser wrote those words in 1958, for the major education-policy backing foundations are, as we have noted, the Gates Foundation and others, though the influence of the Rockefeller and Ford groups remain substantial, as do the ideological goals.

In statements from its documents and studies submitted to the Reece Committee, for example, the Social Science Research Council, a Ford-associated group, called for "a sounder empirical method of research ... to be achieved in political science, if it were to assist in the development of a scientific political control."[61] This was because "an interdependent world is being forced to an awareness of the limitations of individual freedom and personal choice."[62] It takes little imagination to see how Common Core's individually adaptive computerized assessment process fulfills the requirements for those "sounder empirical methods of research" needed to develop "a scientific political control." As we have noted, this quest for "scientific methods" of social engineering have had a tremendous effect in the development and decline of American education, as social scientists have entered the field via foundation support, and via their positioning within the edugarchy and testing "industry," they may, as Wormser noted in a slightly different context, be considered to be a fourth, and largely unaccountable, branch of government.[63] The technocrats', social scientists', and indeed, *any* scientists' or professional group's conformity to the desires and policies of the foundations and the chartered oligarchy that they represent is ensured through the Foundations' grant-giving programs. Money ensures conformity,[64] and in this, one again sees the stimulus-response system of operant conditioning writ large: conformity is rewarded (with grants), nonconformity is punished (with no money and marginalization). One such advocate for foundation power, Frederick P. Keppel, wrote a book in 1950 titled *The Foundation, Its Place in American Life*, in which he proposed that the vast funds available to foundations comprised an enormous pool of "venture capital" for use "in matters concerning welfare and culture."[65]

---

60 Ibid., p. 139.
61 Ibid., p. 95.
62 Ibid., pp. 94–95.
63 René A. Wormser, Foundations: Their Power and Influence, p. 84; see also pp. 90–92.
64 Ibid., p. 140.
65 Ibid., p. 19.

b. Substantive Findings

The specific findings of the Reece Committee as reviewed and analyzed by its general counsel, René Wormser, are an accurate and astute review of the patterns we have seen in evidence in the previous pages, suggesting deep-seated and consistent goals of the edugarchy and their corporate-foundation backers over a prolonged period of time. The foundations and their monies were found being used to advocate for a variety of policy and institutional changes including the following:

1) Discrediting or destruction of entrepreneurial free enterprise;[66] and similarly, that a general "soft" form of collectivization and socialism was consistently promoted;[67]
2) Promoting collective or group enterprises in research and learning over individual study and performance,[68] including promotion of *group review and approval procedures for research projects*;[69]
3) Promotion of foundation-sponsored "professional groups" and journals to function as the "peer review" committees, and hence gatekeepers, of official narratives.[70] In this respect, it is worth noting what the Reece

---

66 René A. Wormser, *Foundations: Their Power and Influence*, p. vii.
67 Ibid., pp. 146, 148. The Reece Committee also noted foundation backing for the radical projects of Columbia Teachers College George S. Counts, whom we have encountered previously, and his calls for teachers to be the change agents "checking the forces of social conservatism and reaction." (p. 153)

    Another collectivist scheme advocated by foundation-sponsored "research" was a plan by the National Association of Secondary School Principals and the National Council for Social Studies, both groups affiliated with the National Education Association. This study recommended that "in order to insure that the public corporations act in accordance with the competitive 'rules of the g/ame,' a special economic court (enjoying the same independence as the courts of justice) might be established... and that the economic court be given the power to repeal any rules of Congress, of legislatures, or of the municipal councils." (pp. 164–165)
68 Ibid., p. 24.
69 Ibid., p. 26.
70 René A. Wormser, op. cit., pp. 42–43. Wormser also observes that a report "produced by Carnegie Corporation money," that of the Commission on Social Studies of the American Historical Association, included a recommendation by Harold J. Laski, a "philosopher of British socialism," which stated in part that "The American Historical Association in cooperation with the National Council on the Social Studies has arranged to take over the magazine, *The Outlook*, as a social science journal for teachers. That writers of textbooks are to be expected to revamp and rewrite their old works in accordance with this frame of reference." (Q.v. pp. 146, 149)

Committee uncovered at some length:

The report of the Reece Committee described the "network of cartels" in the social sciences as having five components. The *first* is a group of foundations, composed of the various Rockefeller and Carnegie foundations, The Ford Foundation (referred to as "a late comer but already partially integrated"), The Commonwealth Fund, The Maurice and Laura Falk Foundation, The Russell Sage Foundation, and others.

The *second component* consists of the "intermediaries" or "clearing houses," such as:

The American Council of Learned Societies
The American Council on Education
The National Academy of Sciences
The National Education Association
The National Research Council
The National Science Foundation
The Social Science Research Council
The Progressive Education Association
The John Dewey Society
The Institute of Pacific Relations
The League for Industrial Democracy
The American Labor Education Service

The learned societies in the several "social sciences" were listed as the *third* component.

The *fourth* consists of the learned journals in these areas.

The *fifth* was "certain individuals in strategic positions, such as certain professors in the institutions which receive the preference of the combine."

The report proceeded:

"*The patterns of interlocking positions* of power may take various shapes. The following are the most frequent ones:
> (1) Trustees of employed executives are successively or simultaneously trustees and executives of several foundations.
> (2) Trustees or executives serve successively or simultaneously as officers of other tax-exempt organizations receiving grants and/or retailing the wholesale grants from their own foundations.

(3) Trustees or executives accept appointments to positions of power in control of education and/or charity so as to multiply their influence beyond the budgetary powers of their foundation resources.

(4) Foundations jointly underwrite major projects, thus arriving at a condition of coordination restraining competition.

(5) Foundations jointly create and support centralized coordinating agencies that operate as instruments of control by claiming supreme authority in a field of education, science, the arts, etc. without any resemblance of democratic representation of the professionals in the management of these agencies.

(6) Rather than distribute money without strings attached, **foundations favor projects of their own and supply the recipient institutions not only with the program, but also with the staff and the detailed operations budget so that the project is actually under control of the foundation, while professionally benefitting from the prestige of the recipient institution. The choice of professors often is one by the foundation and not one by the university.**[71]

Within such a system of interlocking professional groups, journals, and personnel all backed ultimately by foundation funds, the very concept of "peer review" itself becomes grossly distorted and perverted, functioning more as a gatekeeper for approved narratives and policies and thus becoming a central feature of cultural engineering and influence;[72]

---

71 René A. Wormser, *Foundations: Their Power and Influence*, pp. 63–64, italicized emphasis in the original, boldface emphasis added.

72 Wormser observes that "The Committee suggested a special investigation of the extent to which the Social Science Research Council and organization associated with it control book reviews and the literary production—journals, textbooks and other publications—of social scientists. It is a characteristic of the American world of scholarship that academicians are rated largely on their publications, and the test is often quantitative rather than qualitative. Whether or not a social scientist can procure publication of a paper has a lot to do with his advancement in his career. Similarly, the nature of the reviews given to his paper may be of vital importance....

"If, then, control over an academic journal is concentrated in a few hands, it would be easy enough to impose concepts and philosophies on a generation of scholars, and upon school teachers and textbook writers. In more than one instance this had undoubtedly happened. Such control may take the form of denying space to a nonconformist. It may also influence commercial publishers

4) The interlock of foundations with professional groups and councils often manifests itself in a very different way, with a professional group or council effectively "fronting" for the support of a variety of foundations cooperating for a particular goal. In this respect, the Reece Committee drew attention to the fact that the American Council on Education was backed by a constellation of foundations, including the Rockefeller General Education Board, the Carnegie Corporation, the Carnegie Endowment for International Peace, the Carnegie Foundation for the Advancement of Teaching, and the Ford Fund for Adult Education, among many others;[73]

5) The foundation support for professional organizations and journals was also extended to encompass an influence over school private and public accrediting agencies themselves;[74]

6) The foundations exhibited a consistent pattern of support for internationalist or globalist policies, positions, and institutions,[75] and these policies, positions, and institutions were advocated by a similar interlocking network of professional journals and groups, behind which stood the same grouping of foundations as exhibited in education;[76]

7) Given these ideological positions and commitments, it was also necessary for this interlocking group of foundations and the dynastic capital they represented to infiltrate major American academic business and management departments and faculties with similar stimulus-response, operant conditioning and collectivist techniques and policies, beginning with the Ford Foundation's influence over the Harvard Graduate School of Business Administration;[77]

---

via the expert readers to whom books are submitted before publication. It is very likely that these experts would be selected from those favored by the journal. Publishers may be reluctant to publish a nonconformist's book because the conformists, articulate and welcomed in the pages of a professional journal, may pan it with unfavorable reviews or freeze it out of circulation by withholding reviews in the controlled learned journals and in book-review sections." (pp. 72–73)

73 René A. Wormser, *Foundations: Their Power and Influence*, p. 76. The Reece Committee also pointed out the foundation influence behind the funding of the Ruggs textbook recommendations and Ruggs textbooks themselves, and for Abraham Flexner's progressive "Lincoln" school which influenced the development of the Ruggs textbooks. (See pp. 157, 160–161)

74 Wormser, op. cit., p. 142.

75 Ibid., p. 200

76 Ibid., p. 202.

77 Ibid., pp. 284–285.

8) This issued in yet another pattern of interlock, that between foundations, education, and universities (particularly in education and business
faculties).[78]

c. Methodological Findings

In addition to these substantive findings of the goals and policies advocated
by foundations as evidenced in their funding and grants to certain special
projects, as well as their sponsorship of certain professional gatekeeping
groups and journals, the Reece Committee also discovered a consistent
pattern of operational tactics in advancing their aims, some of which we
have already encountered in previous chapters. Among the most prominent
patterns it discovered, ones which we have seen in abundant evidence in the
progressivist edugarchy and their foundation backing, are the following:

1) Interlocking personnel, i.e., personnel serving simultaneously in foundations and in professional associations or foundation-funded projects,
or alternatively, moving quickly from foundations to professional associations and foundation-funded projects, and then back to foundations, in
quick succession, including such simultaneous service or quick-succes-
sion service between foundations and government agencies;[79]

2) The consistent tactic of presenting the policies or positions which they
advocate as "inevitable" or "inevitable change,"[80] a euphemistic way of
stating that opposition is futile;

3) The deliberate use of euphemistic ambiguities to cloak and promote
public acceptance, while allowing the pursuit of radical policies, i.e.,
presenting to the foundation boards and to the general public "a program
so general as to get approval and yet so indefinite as to permit activities
which in the judgment of competent critics are either wasteful or harmful
to the education program which has been approved by the public."[81]

4) A variation of this tactic is simply to use traditional language and
terms which have a publicly agreed-upon general meaning or cultural
significance, but which have been redefined or invested with radically

---

78 Ibid., p. 23.
79 René A. Wormser, *Foundations: Their Power and Influence*, pp. 59–60.
80 Ibid., See, for example, the comments on p. 146.
81 Ibid., p. 254.

different meanings by the professional cliques using them. The classic example cited by the Reece Committee's general counsel is the technique of redefining "inalienable rights" not in terms of an equality before the law, but as freedom from various social or economic ills, as defined by that very clique itself.[82]

Given the range and depth of its investigations and findings, perhaps it is not surprising that in 1953, as the Reece Committee began its investigation work by trying to build on the work of its predecessor the Cox Committee, it discovered that much of the Cox Committee's files had mysteriously disappeared, and it was never determined whether Cox Committee staff members had simply destroyed them, or whether they had been stolen.[83]

Given all these findings, it should come as no surprise that there is an even *murkier* connection lurking in the background.

4. The Dirtiest Connection: The Edugarchy, Mind Control, the National Security State and the Surveillance Culture

Catherine Austin Fitts, former Assistant Secretary of Housing and Urban Development during the administration of President George Herbert Walker Bush, has observed that Obamacare and Common Core constitute two poles of the same mechanism, a mechanism which in turn is designed with two principal objectives in mind: firstly, to harness the last remaining pockets of local wealth in health and education, and secondly, to extend to the level of the individual the surveillance state's apparatus and ability to monitor, and hence to influence if not control, the individual's health, and emotional, cultural, and intellectual life.

Here too, the contemporary situation is the product of a long historical association and development between the edugarchy and the national security state, for during the 1950s, Henry Chauncey's Educational Testing Service conducted no fewer than seven studies under a contract for the Society for the Investigation of Human Ecology. This "society" was, however, a CIA front, and the studies it contracted out to the Educational Testing Service were for its

---

82 Ibid., p. 260.
83 René A. Wormser, *Foundations: Their Power and Influence*, p. 335.

notorious MKULTRA mind control program.[84] In this respect, it is worth noting that the postwar MKULTRA program and its connection to "professional educational testing" was itself the possible product of earlier relationships developed during World War II, for Harvard president James Bryant Conant, whom we have encountered earlier in these pages in respect to his own agendas for the utilization of education as a sorting mechanism for the creation of a new aristocracy of merit, was the head during the war of the National Defense Research Committee. One special division within this committee, Division 19, was established to create tools and techniques of psychological warfare and hence, of mind manipulation.[85] Many of these CIA grants came in the euphemistic form of grants to study "human ecology." Additionally, the CIA front the Society for the Investigation of Human Ecology also disbursed $140,000 to David Saunders of the Educational Testing Service,[86] ostensibly for the purpose of creating national variations of personality tests.

The Society for the Investigation of Human Ecology's own interests are revealed to be entirely in line with Henry Chauncey's desire to turn the Educational Testing Service into a massive testing and sorting agency (and, one suspects, an indoctrination agency), for in December, 1960, it issued a report called *Brainwashing: A Guide to the Literature*.[87] Alan W. Scheflin and Edward M. Opton, Jr., co-authors of the now-classic study of the CIA's mind control projects, *The Mind Manipulators*, observe that the Society for the Investigation of Human Ecology was a front established for the purpose of funneling "money to researchers while concealing the fact that the CIA was the source of those funds."[88] The fact that the ETS' Saunders apparently *knew* this fact is interesting and suggestive, for it implies that at some deep level, the standardized testing industry is less about accurate or "objective" evalua-

---

84 Nicholas Lemann, *The Secret History of the American Meritocracy*, p. 90. Lemann's observation is worth noting: "But ETS did perform seven studies to a CIA front called the Society for the Investigation of Human Ecology. These were part of a CIA project called MKULTRA, which is best known for having administered LSD to unwitting subjects, one of whom jumped out of a window and died, but which from the ETS point of view was one of the few sponsors it ever found for its personality research."

85 John Marks, *The Search for the "Manchurian Candidate": The CIA and Mind Control: The Secret History of the Behavioral Sciences* (New York: W.W. Norton and Company, 1991), p. 14.

86 John Marks, *The Search for the "Manchurian Candidate,"* p. 179.

87 Alan W. Scheflin and Edward M. Opton, Jr., *The Mind Manipulators* (New York: Paddington Press, Ltd., 1978), p. 90.

88 Ibid., p. 143.

tion of an individual's academic performance, and more about measuring the degree of successful indoctrination of that individual. It is, as we have argued, a tool of social engineering and governance, and not of education at all.

In addition to this, in 1947 the National Training Laboratory was founded, designed to explore patterns of human behavior and relations. The members and founders of this laboratory in many instances either served with, or had connections to, the USA's World War II intelligence service, the Office of Strategic Services (OSS).[89] In 1962, this "laboratory" published a book, *Five Issues in Training*, spelling out how individuals could have their entire worldview "unfrozen, changed, and then refrozen" again. Noting that "The Chinese communists would remove the target person from those situations and social relationships which tended to confirm and reinforce the validity of the old attitudes,"[90] the process consists of conducting retreats and/or workshops where individuals are then pressured to perform activities designed to "unfreeze" their attitudes, inject new ones, and freeze them again. In such activities, the "facilitator"—our fictitious "Robert/a" whom we previously encountered—becomes the principal change agent in a series of passive-aggressive "learning activities" all designed around "cooperative learning" and the suppression of the individual.[91]

These social engineering and national security state surveillance patterns are echoed decades later in remarks that Bill Gates made in 2005 to a national conference of state governors. There, Gates stressed the now standard memes that America's high schools had to be completely "reinvented" because they were obsolete. The "fix," of course, was to expand the role of technology not only for instructional purposes, but more importantly, "for monitoring and collecting standardizing data on student assessments, and for developing large-scale integrated longitudinal databases on student and teacher performance."[92] A database tracking all individual student and teacher performances "longitudinally," i.e., through time, constitutes an extraordinary tool of surveillance, and such a database would be of enormous financial value to the corporations administering it, since such a database would

---

89 Charlotte Thomson Iserbyt, *The Deliberate Dumbing Down of America*, p. 55.

90 Ibid., citing *Five Issues in Training* (National Training Laboratory), p. 49.

91 Ibid., p. 63. Thomson Iserbyt notes that this movement toward "cooperative learning" and "group projects" and even group grades was yet another product of the University of Columbia Teachers College, and hence is another product of the Wundtian Succession.

92 Anthony G. Picciano and Joel Spring, *The Great American Education-Industrial Complex: Ideology, Technology, and Profit* (New York: Routledge, 2013), p. 137.

give invaluable insight into trending market choices, a veritable goldmine of insider trading information. For the government, such a database would constitute the ultimate tool for refining and perfecting social engineering and control mechanisms. The real "fix" here is the mercantilist policy, for the promotion of technology through foundation money benefits those corporations marketing educational "technology" to begin with. Given this fact, it is reasonable to question whether the real goals have anything whatsoever to do with improving education at either the level of content or instruction, since the real agendas appear to be consonant with Playfair's observations with which we began this chapter, for the real agendas are profits for the few, and the installation of a mechanism of social influence and surveillance.

Indeed, in this respect, the Gates Foundation appears to epitomize the educational-industrial complex, and yet another pattern of the way foundations operate that we have seen emerge in the historical record: the infiltration of personnel into agencies of government.[93] Anthony G. Picciano and Joel Spring point out that James Shelton, current Assistant Deputy Secretary for Education Innovation and Improvement, worked with the Gates Foundation "for almost 8 years,"[94] while yet another Gates Foundation individual, Margot Rogers, on the staff of Education Secretary Arne Duncan, had served the Gates Foundation in the development of its education strategy, and served its "education division's investment committee and strategic leadership team."[95] When Rogers left the U.S. Department of Education in 2011, she was replaced by Joanne Weiss, "who was a partner at the New Schools Venture Fund, which received tens of millions of dollars from the Gates Foundation."[96] This revolving door between the foundation and corporate world and government agencies have led some to observe that the Department of Education is, to some extent, a front for the Gates Foundation.[97] In effect, the foundation-education complex is a shadow governance mechanism, one which, in the hands of the Gates Foundation, is advocating the removal of traditional union protections regarding teacher-layoff policies and sweeping changes in teacher evaluation.[98]

---

93 Anthony G. Picciano and Joel Spring, *The Great American Education-Industrial Complex: Ideology, Technology, and Profit* (New York: Routledge, 2013), p. 136.
94 Ibid., p. 136.
95 Ibid., pp. 136–137, quotation from p. 137.
96 Ibid., p. 137.
97 Ibid.
98 Ibid., p. 21.

In other words, Common Core is but the extension of the patterns that we have seen within the edugarchy since the late nineteenth century. It is a mechanism of corporate governance and control enabled by the advent of the Internet and computer technologies and databases. This American mechanism is plugged into even wider mechanisms of the edugarchy, such as the World Economic Forum, which circulates reports and positions papers on educational policy which "might be considered a reflection of network discussions about education that are 'sound' and acceptable to the global elite."[99]

And lurking in the shadows on the edges and beneath it all are all the agencies of corrupt covert power and surveillance, which have not hesitated to blend their covert operations, social engineering, and mind control research, and to recruit the institutions of educational power and influence to do so. If nothing else, this should highlight the fact that the real problem behind Common Core is *not* the common-sense idea that there should be some canonical standard of academic content, but rather that the individually adaptive computerized assessment process itself, with all its inherent dangers for abuse, including the massive concentration of power in the hands of anonymous test preparers, psychologists, social engineers, and corporate database managers, is the real rotten heart of Common Core.

---

99 Ibid., p. 33.

"More" is Neither
Better nor Necessary

---

*"Although these findings haven't been widely publicized, studies of student responses of different ages have found **a statistical association between high scores on standardized tests and relatively shallow thinking.**"*

*"Students are unable to **generate** a response; all they can do is recognize one by picking it out of four or five answers provided by someone else. They can't even **explain** their reasons for choosing the answer they did."*

—

ALFIE KOHN[1]

As we conclude our larger picture analysis of how we got to where we are, we leave the reader with some practical considerations for the immediate problems in the local school. We would encourage parents and grandparents, as well as concerned citizens, to take careful notes which might prove helpful in making immediate local changes in schools where the wheels have nearly flown off the educational wagon.

A. The Modern Classroom

Does more *really* equal more? Objectively speaking with regard to the face value of the statement, clearly the answer is yes. However, the public school

---

1   Alfie Kohn, *The Case Against Standardized Testing: Raising the Scores, Ruining the Schools* (Portsmouth, NH: Heineman, 2000), pp. 10, 11, respectively, emphasis in the original.

system has accepted this concept without following its own methodology of reassessment, for it is in practical terms often to be answered in the negative. The issue is not minutes, days, months, assignments, group-work, homework, technology, teacher training sessions, etc., but rather, *what must be put under the academic microscope is the flawed philosophy which has spread like a cancer into the body of American public school education. Quality,* not quantity, *should be measured and reexamined,* beginning with the educational theorists and education departments and certification requirements themselves.

As with all things, statistics can be used, i.e. manipulated, to prove or disprove any presupposition. The reader is therefore encouraged to review the many reports which are readily available online regarding traditional school calendars, year-round schools, block scheduling, four-day school weeks, and the results as to the effectiveness of time in school and achievements. (The following observations, criticisms and recommendations are those of co-author Gary Lawrence, and may be taken as objective or subjective depending on how one takes such observations—and each reader will find a statistic embedded in the "latest study" by well-funded "experts" to support or oppose these observations.) There is a reason I am choosing to avoid that circular reasoning defense of these "studies"; I have conducted my own and it is from that standpoint alone that I write.

I offer my observations as one who has been in the classroom for multiple decades; I have taught in rural *and* urban schools; I have been awarded with certificates from the local districts where I have taught and have set professional teacher benchmarks in the state where I am credentialed. I hold multiple degrees, finished *summa cum laude* in my undergraduate studies and earned a doctorate as well. Thus, my own *expert opinion* in this case ought to suffice for any need the reader feels at this point forward to understand that my conclusions are based on decades of professional observations; this, I propose as my supporting evidence.

B. More of **What?**

Typically, an average student in a public school will attend 180 days of school and approximately 1,200 hours will be logged in. How those hours are broken down vary, but in the majority of public high schools the average class is fifty-five minutes, and six classes are attended each day. A teacher is expected to handle administrative tasks such as taking attendance and handing out call slips during class, tasks which should not require more than five minutes of lost time, aside from the occasional announcements that interrupt the class. During the remaining forty-five to fifty minutes of class time what can be accomplished?

An effective teacher knows that instructional time is limited but where one teacher sees limitations, another teacher sees opportunities and squeezes each second of each minute into transformative learning moments. Well thought-out and planned lessons are launched without delay, barbed with hooks to reach nearly every student, and are layered or "scaffolded" with informative and attention-holding lectures, learning examples, and the best audio-visual aids available. Students are accustomed to forty-five minutes staring at a television and rarely lose attention. How are the same forty-five minutes in a classroom less an opportunity to change a life by instruction? The truth is, forty-five minutes sitting in front of a sitcom are passed far quicker than forty-five minutes in front of infomercials advertising the latest innovation in garden hoses.

C. Ineffective Solutions Offered:
1. More Time

Time is not the critical factor; intelligence, *passion* and communication on the part of the teacher are! To see why, just perform a simple thought experiment: Imagine yourself sitting silently through nearly *seven lackluster hours* with a disinterested and ill-prepared salesman hawking a product you see no personal need or want for. Worse yet, the salesman himself has little interest in creating that need for the product that he knows little about and is being paid to push on you. (He knows little about it, because he has spent more time in education and certification courses and continuing education workshops, learning more about the latest methodological educational fad or gimmick, than he has about the discipline he is supposed to teach.) This seven-hour endurance exercise is followed by a test in which you are forced to regurgitate the information back under penalty of having to repeat the same information a second time, five days a week. Now you will begin to understand that time is less the problem than the instructor. *The student is a hostage to the ineffective teacher or is an engaged participant who dreads to hear the next bell while in the presence of an effective teacher.*

Time ticks away slowly as minutes feel like hours in one class and like a blink of the eye in the other. Days, weeks, months pass like an eternity or like nanoseconds depending on the teacher. Effective teaching can be gauged by the teacher-student learning rapport (measurable in assessments as well) more accurately than the days on a calendar or minutes on a clock. When a student is interested in learning, it creates the passion and desire to learn more, and every moment is thereafter treasured. It is the teacher who too often fails to engage the student with the interest to learn. A clock, a homework assignment, and a test do not inspire a desire to learn! A personal reflection may suffice: most of my students will return to me at the end of their fourth year in high school with the comment, "I learned more in that one year in your class than I did in all of my years combined before and afterwards." How can this be unless time is assessed by quality rather than quantity?

The multitude of studies, as previously recommended to be reviewed by the reader, suggests various findings regarding length of minutes per class, length of days per year, best months and best hours for learning, and at the same time concluding that the studies are largely difficult to make absolute sense of, as findings vary from state to state, district to district, school to school. I suggest that the answer to this riddle is in *the area that is truly the X factor: the teacher*, and *not* the amount or the arrangement of the time spent in the classroom. Undoubtedly more time with an effective teacher is more beneficial than less time with that teacher. Likewise, less time with an ineffective teacher would certainly boost morale among students and hardly change learning results in ineffective classrooms.

Unfortunately this X factor is not considered when districts or states sit down to solve the problem of lower scores and dropping attendance rates among students. More time is always a standard answer and the only restraining factor in adding even *more* time is the expense of having to pay teachers more money or face a walk-out or strike for longer hours at the same pay.

2. More Homework

Again, more hours must mean higher learning will be the result. Again, false! A student who does not understand a lesson during the fifty minutes of instruction is not going to suddenly discover the hidden nugget of truth at home. Why? Common sense supplies the obvious answers.

1) Parents generally work longer hours or multiple jobs and have little time or energy after work to prepare a meal, unwind, and then review a

handout (often without instruction or examples) covering material that they learned a decade ago or more in their own past.

2) Many students are caretakers for brothers or sisters and are occupied in helping the parents care for siblings. This is simply the reality in our present society and the economic demand most two-working-parent families deal with.

3) The student, if left to accomplish the task *without* parental support, and who did *not* understand the material in class, is less likely to do anything other than reinforce mistakes or give up in frustration. The reward the following day in class is one more F grade on an assignment sent home without necessary support to learn. At this point the teacher and administrator will suggest point 4, after-school tutoring:

4) After-school tutoring is a blessing for a small fraction of students who have the luxury to stay after school and try to learn what was not learned or completed in class. The downside is that in most districts, students ride the bus home, and the bus does not adjust its schedule for a student to stay in school another hour. Parents cannot leave work to pick up their child as most are working, and the after-school solution benefits very few students given the transportation problems associated with it.

5) Nearly seven hours in school, sitting at a desk, is as exhausting on a teenager or pre-adolescent as it is on any adult who has spent the same amount of time at work. Downtime is critical and pushing the limits into additional time in the evening rarely results in more than short-term memorization, if anything at all is to be achieved or hoped for. The parent who brings work home into the evening and weekend is far more likely to choose what lesser priority must be sacrificed: marriage, children, chores, health. If parents are well aware of this, why are teachers (who are often parents as well) so blind to this reality?

What then is to be done regarding homework? Am I suggesting all homework must be forbidden? No. Rather, I offer a balanced view as an alternative to black-and-white, all-or-nothing fallacies. Some students will require more time to *complete* assignments and must use the time at home for this purpose. Note carefully, the *completion* of work which the teacher had time to assign *and assist* students during class is more likely to be completed at home and be understood, thereby making homework productive and reinforcing learned material. This ought to be the rule for homework. At this point, perhaps it is good to remind any teachers still reading this book that you are not the only teacher the student has and if *each* teacher sends home a single hour of homework four nights a week, a student is now at home with a minimum of four to five hours of homework per night! I wonder how many teachers take four to five hours' worth of student papers home to grade per evening each day?

What of projects which are often assigned over weeks or months and also become "homework"? Once again, if properly thought through before being assigned by the teacher, the student has time with the teacher during the weeks or months before the project is due to ask for clarification. Such a project also allows for periodic review of the student's work in progress, and nothing is expected at home overnight during which time the student did not have ample time to have added instruction and gradual correction toward completion.

To hit one last nail on the head: we must ask, as a society built on the family at the core of instruction in formal education and morality, whether time at the table with the family for dinner or time together on weekends, or setting aside a day for worship, is to be replaced by a child sitting with an open book for hours after school, on weekends, and more often than not falling asleep without having had family time, personal downtime, and mental rest? Could a lack of sleep, lack of family time, and a lack of relaxation be contributing causes to teen depression in the name of *more* hours of "learning"? One must wonder. The research-minded reader will find statistics to validate that rhetorical question. One academic study provides convincing evidence that short-term memory (most of what students learn in school fifty-five minutes at a time) is not only limited but it is most effective early in the morning, and as the day grows on less and less is retained! This study alone raises serious questions about the effectiveness of using "homework" as a learning activity for young students.[2]

3. More Summer Assignments

It has become fashionable, under the guise of *more* learning (without the burden of teacher hours and pay), to give summer assignments to students. Simply stated, *the instruction is absent but the appearance of more time is sup-*

---

2   (Professor George Miller, Psychological Review, 1956). Burton, Kate; Ready, Romilla (2009-09-03).

plied. A student who *is* able to learn without formal instruction may sadly prove the very thing teachers are most afraid of—the redundancy of a teacher in the role of learning. The objection to this argument is predictable and I have heard it more than once when debating the value of a summer assignment: it is not to *teach new* material but rather to keep students active in the learning process during the eight to ten weeks away from the classroom. I question the purpose and value of this policy, as one who believes that time around the table for a meal during the school year is a critical component of child-adolescent learning; so likewise time with the family to vacation, to take day and evening walks, to share in hobbies and outdoor activities is far more productive than an assignment *not* intended to instruct but to *occupy time.* In my experience as a teacher, the percentage of students who actually do the assignments over summer is a minority and those who do it well are a rare few. Without guidance, instruction, and a purpose worth pursuing, added assignments do not result in more learning. Thus, many students are punished with an immediate lower grade on the first day of school and the assignment fails to prove its worth as a time obligation or an assessment for the teacher on the first day of school after a summer break.

4. More "Group Work"

(N.B.: I am directing the following critique pointedly and solely toward the educational philosophy which is thrust on teachers during credentialing, professional developments, and imposed through local school "professional learning communities." Some districts and schools are more accommodating, while others employ overbearing administrators who dictate how lessons are to be taught and how classrooms are to be arranged. This critique is **not** aimed at occasional instances for variation in strategies or convenient opportunities during which individual teachers sparingly choose to make use of putting students in pairs or groups, i.e., debates, group projects during in which each student receives **an individual grade for his or her own work**, etc.)

As Communism drifts into the dustbins of history, the American spirit of rugged individualism and achievement struggles to define itself as worthy of having a place in the modern-world public school curriculum. Shared achievement and group discoveries play a more active role in education and are encouraged as more effective learning strategies. The key to reaching all students, we are taught in modern American teacher credentialing, is the group model. The pride of possessing an idea must give way toward the greater social need of sharing ideas, relying on others for consensus, and advancing societal aims. Engineering a common mind requires community thinking, community solutions, and community agreement.

However, the trend to have *more* group activities in order to achieve greater learning outcomes is one more example where "more equals less." The desk has given way to the "group-table-designed classroom" and the "teacher" has become the "facilitator" for peer to educate peer in group work. It has all the advantages of sounding progressive, but there is a fallacy to "more group work equates to more learning."

The weakest link in the chain determines the strength of the overall chain, and in many classrooms it is imagined that the weaker link is strengthened by the stronger link of group work. However, ask any advanced student regarding the effectiveness of this ideology, and that student will shrug and admit that they are held back at the expense of the struggling student in the group. Typically, the stronger becomes weaker while the weakest is only artificially held in place as if by their own improved strength. *Any assessment thereafter given to the **individual** will reveal the flaws in this strategy.* Left to himself, the student fails. Is this therefore proof that all must work together to succeed? Or is it rather an indictment that in the name of "community" we have carelessly abandoned the actual progress of an individual to stand on his or her own in the present and future? Education's aim ought not to be the creation of a society of dependents, but rather to support each individual through instruction and mastery of how to become self-reliant, while also respectful of the unique gifts that others must rely on for success in their life callings also.

Each student must climb their own academic ladder and some will reach farther than others, though all are capable of climbing to the greatest limits within their personal abilities. An effective teacher, not a Scantron test, will assess the student individually and recognize handicaps to advancement in that student. Some students are lagging due to laziness while others suffer from learning disabilities, and yet others require more visual, more hands-on, repetition, and so on, but the effective teacher will both recognize and apply an appropriate adjustment to break through, and encourage each student to find it within themselves to grow step by step toward their potential. To move all students together is only a guarantee that the climbing purpose of the ladder must be jettisoned for the greater good of climbing together; community purpose supersedes the goal of any single student climbing beyond the limits previously set by one before them, and fails the student as well as society.

Is there, then, no place for collaboration among students, shared projects among students, pairing opportunities, or groups? Indeed there is. As with most corrections to a problem, the answer is not necessarily arrived at by an all-or-nothing option, it is solved by (1) an acknowledgment in the fallacy imbedded in the primary strategy that students will achieve higher learning in groups rather than as singular learners, and (2) by adjusting assessments any time group or pairings occur. Each student must be held accountable for specific tasks and each individual student alone must receive a grade for his or her quality of work contributed. Too often a "group grade" is given which is a punishment to the student striving for the best work and grade. Every experienced teacher knows that the best student will complete the work for the lower performing student as well as himself or herself in such cases in order to make sure the group grade does not punish him or her.

"But someday this student must learn this because in the real world and on the job, working together is the reality," the critic will reply. Indeed, and if the "team" has lost an important contract because one team member failed to execute his or her particular responsibilities, that employee will be fired and replaced by a "team worker," i.e., a worker who *does* his or her *own* part for the good of the team. *Again, each student or employee stands or falls on individual accomplishments and it is extremely rare that an entire department in any professional field is fired for the failure of a single individual.*

Consider the following thought experiment: How often has *every* member of a losing team in professional sports been released for a losing season? It is counterproductive to fire effective workers or players who only suffer the underperformance of their colleagues. More often than not, the effective worker releases himself (i.e., leaves the place of employment) in order to be free from the bondage of the incompetent, and to place himself in a better environment that allows him to work to his full potential! A final note to administrators and district board members: if you are losing the best teachers in your schools and districts, it is most likely a sign that your best teachers are frustrated by the professional whirlpool of incompetence spiraling downward, hindering them from reaching their potential personally and with their students.

5. More Technology

Technology is a great benefit to mankind and has become indispensable with regard to productivity. A computer can calculate, retain information, and gather results to simple or advanced inquiries at lightning speed, making it appear to be the ultimate weapon in the war against ignorance. For the savvy student the computer is more than a best friend, it can format a paper, research information, spell-check, and virtually write a paper through copy-and-paste commands!

The computer, with the slightest amount of human interference or wasted time, can generate tests, grade the tests, and store the information in a database for the local district, state, or federal departments seeking access to such valuable information. Making sense of that information is a matter for the "experts" to use, or in order to tweak or program the system and pass along to the local educators in the latest and greatest updated version of the standardized test. Naturally this eliminates all of the messy subjective problems that occur in education when humans teach, learn, and have to be assessed. One might therefore ask, why not allow the computer to do the teaching as well as the assessments? Indeed, why not?

And thus we arrive at yet another rottenness at the heart of Common Core.

There has been a movement in public education—commensurate with the introduction of Common Core Standards—to introduce tablets or laptops into the hands of each student from elementary to high school. In the infancy of this movement the student and teacher largely used the technology to read together from e-books, conduct simple searches, take tests, and read supplemental material (supplemental because text*books* were still the standard for teacher and student learning in K–12). It did not take long before textbook companies realized the trend away from paper and began the process to turn the physical textbook into a digital textbook. The World Wide Web linked to a textbook could suddenly supply archival video footage, research links, biographies, audio readings of speeches or poetry, etc., What was not to celebrate under the banner of "more technology leads to more learning"?

Again, more does not necessarily lead to the desired result of higher learning. More information available does not guarantee that the student understands more; it only supplies *easy* access to information which is far too often copied, pasted, and in the grand scheme of time the student (and teacher) trade off "critical thinking education" for "type, search, click, copy and paste education." One key sacrifice is time *lost* for reflection of the material under the presumed benefit that expediency wins the day.

To put it simply, what is lost, at the cost of saving time at the worshipped feet of technology, is time for the student to *think*!

But to think what? For starters: What does this information really mean? Why is this information significant? Is this particular accumulation of material so quickly reached without effort even *relevant* or *accurate* information? What information has been neglected and why? Who determined that this information is the only information necessary and where would one find contradictory or supplemental information that is not stored on the Internet? Archimedes' all-important *"aha! Eureka!"* moment is lost, and worse yet, it isn't even understood by the student that such a thing exists! The speed of information is improved while the educational outcome of true scholarship is as extinct as the dinosaur (and traditional teacher).

If the Internet and digital lessons are the generals leading the troops to educational victory, one must trust them without stopping to ask insubordinate questions such as "why?" The key assessments, particularly those designed to be associated with Common Core Standards, are the measuring stick of a student's learning which has been supplied by digital lessons, digital textbooks, and digital assignments. At what point does the student realize that the human sitting at the desk surfing the Internet is a proctor and the real teacher is digital also? In most classrooms the students are well aware of this fact already; it is the teachers who are slow to realize this fact while sleeping under their security blanket of tenure.[3] Where are the teachers, unions, and administration in protest to such a future destined to take away their profession? They are not the protestors, they are the advocates!

Already in some states, a student can enroll in a public school education without stepping foot into a physical classroom or having face-to-face contact with an educator. Presently some of the programs in these states supplement the home-online learning (at grades elementary–8) with textbooks and handouts, but it is through the online educational program that the student is able to receive a full, and tuition-free, public school education, without the need

---

[3]   In a recent article posted at dianeravitch.net *it appears that New York State has already been so bold as to set into motion an instructional-assessment technology ideology: "Most educators agree that the current LECTURE-STYLE (emphasis added) approach to teaching is flawed ...this approach limits the teacher's ability to adapt his or her classroom to meet a number of 21st-century teaching needs such as INDIVIDU-ALIZED AND PERSONALIZED INSTRUCTION (emphasis added), personalized learning, competency-based grouping and progression, seamless blending of instruction and assessment, and timely impact of assessment results to affect instruction." This appeared after the first draft of the present book was being written predicting this very dangerous dystopia educational future! dianeravitch.net/2015/11/06/tim-farley-the-frightening-plans-for-new-york-competency-based-education-or-embedded-testing/*

of personal instruction by an "educator" to lecture, assess, *and ask critical thinking questions.* The student is, as the program itself, *input and output only.* It is therefore also not surprising that key funding with political agendas drive this new wave of public education which saves the state unnecessary expenses such as building new schools or paying for new teachers. It is a financial win-win situation with computer-generated assessments to prove its effectiveness in "education." Who can argue with such results?

We are now past the point of no return, and through the delusion of more technology equals more learning, we are creating a future society in which the computer handles the former function of the human brain. Critical thinking, once the aim of education, is as passé as chalk and student chalkboards. The student brain is trained by ritual and practice in the art of mental *submission*; the student's brain is a modern servant collecting and recycling the superior electronic brain's information. Although the student is not entirely passive nor the technology entirely active, the roles are well established by superiority and inferiority.

The outcomes do in fact appear that education is more a human passive and computer active reality. Basic knowledge in writing skills, spelling, grammar, formatting a letter versus a short story, etc., is better left in the portable laptop than the confines of a human skull. Dates, names, places, etc., associated with history or geography, are safer in the memory of "the cloud" than in the brain.

If the strategy of modern education is an effective use of type, search, seek, and find, then the role of the teacher has changed with it, though that memo has not yet been sent or has accidentally found its way to the junk filter through the district e-mail settings. The modern "teacher," such a memo might read, is one who supervises the proper steps in collecting predetermined Internet or digital information, toward the objective of recycling it through further high-level knowledge required in applying the proper command necessary in order for the machine to format and send to the "teacher" via e-mail, text, Google Classroom, or printer. One can only imagine how long it will take before the printer goes the way of the vellum, quill and inkwell!

I predict with more and more technology in place and provided by "experts" in the form of standardized lessons and assessments for the student based on his or her scores gathered from the previous computer-generated assessment, the modern classroom teacher will be a relic of the past and serve only as an occasional proctor in the presence of students sent to a physical learning center, or will be the distance adjunct tutor or supervisor for the online public school student.

6. More Teacher Workshops and Professional Development

Following on from the previous point, it is not far-fetched to begin arguing that the problem is the teacher and not the student. "*Hear, hear,*" the parents reply! "*Our children are as smart today as when we were children, the problem must be the teachers.*" Well, yes *and* no. I have already supplied more than a few criticisms of the failures that are to be laid near the feet of the teacher for flawed strategies in the classroom and therefore will not directly add to the growing list of teacher failures in this point. At each previous point, what I have pointed to was a strategy or philosophical problem used by the teacher, a strategy or philosophy that the teacher has been taught and is often given a professional evaluation for instituting in their classroom! Some teachers buy into the strategies and philosophies while others recognize that flying under the administrative radar means knowing that their job performance is based on using (often modifying) the strategies, and remaining silent when the administrators or district coaches sing praises of worship to the latest modern philosophy or methodology. Naturally, those few teachers who speak out or do not participate in such group decisions are labeled and ostracized for not being "team" players.

Like everything else in modern education, initials and acronyms supply the answer: more "PDs" or "professional developments" for teachers, more workshops and conferences on site and occasionally off-site in resort cities such as Las Vegas, Monterey, Boston, etc.—all expenses paid, of course. For the average hard-working parent the off-site resort conferences probably seem an unnecessary waste of money at the taxpayers' expense, and I heartily agree. I have attended more than a few that were quite useful in research for this chapter, while an utter waste of time as a professional teacher. What follows are, once again, my observations and accurate reports for those who have not been *privileged* to sit in on these sessions.

7. On-Site "Professional Development"

Generally, each year the teachers are called to the district or to the local school auditorium for these mandatory learning sessions; few would ever volunteer to attend if they were optional. What follows is a district coach, or team of coaches who have prepared the room with tables for a set number of teachers to sit together in groups. With each group table is a large poster-sized paper, markers, and package of Post-It notes. Immediately one understands the concept of "modeling," as coaches are "modeling" for the teachers how to give a proper and effective lesson. In some instances each teacher is expected to fill out a "Hello my name is ..." label so that when called upon, the coach can be both specific and give an air of interest in that teacher. A predictable PowerPoint presentation is lit up and the show is on. Statistics, charts, and the occasional poorly told joke is inserted. Interestingly, these often take place "after school," which raises the ire of teachers who complain (as their students) that they have been working all day and hardly have time or interest to sit through two hours of boring material put on by disinterested and disconnected commissars who don't understand the real problems or needs in their classes.

In keeping with the strategy being used for effectively engaging all learners, after a certain amount of instructional time, the teachers are given a group assignment for which all materials have been supplied on the group table. While the teachers work together sharing ideas and reaching a consensus on how best to summarize and regurgitate the information on the poster board, the commissars walk the room and ask questions or make comments: *"interesting," "nice use of colors," "well done," "what does this skull and crossbones flag represent from the lesson?"*

Finally, the *coup de grâce*, the portrait gallery walk! Yes, the groups must paste their poster on a wall for a parade of teachers to walk past, as if in a museum of fine arts. As each group walks by, they pause, study it, place hand under chin to look scholarly, and mutter, *"hmmm... ah yes... quite... indeed..."* and after an appointed time (supplied by a bell or chime) each group moves to the next mundane display.

Two hours later the coaches feel satisfied, and the teachers feel insulted and resentful for having lost two hours of their valuable after-school relaxation time. Any failure now to reach higher scores by students in the classrooms of these well-instructed teachers must be laid at the feet of the teachers; the commissars have satisfied their obligations, and the chain of blame is firmly in place. Coaches can blame teachers, teachers can blame students, parents can blame the system, and student scores rarely show improvement and more often than not reveal a decline in comparison to other civilized industrial nations throughout the world. The modeling is effectively reinforcing a vicious cycle of failure in the classroom.

8. Off-Site Conferences for "Professional Development"

The Setting: Who would not want an all-expenses-paid week vacation/conference in Las Vegas, San Diego, Monterey, Colorado Springs, Miami, or Boston? Buffets, free time, drinks at the local watering hole in the evening, and time on the beach, in the casino, or at the showroom? It is a guaranteed good time for all in the name of professional development. The best of the best provide the sessions located in various conference rooms throughout the day, with a keynote speaker each morning after the buffet breakfast. The largest room is reserved for tables set up by the companies sponsoring the conference with an assortment of free T-shirts, pens, keychains, and stickers which abound for the teacher to take back in the custom nylon bag provided free of charge.

The Content: Keynote speakers have the greater share of the morning session with full video, audio, spotlights, and book tables selling their information in the rear of the auditorium. The keynote address is often the theme of the conference which is focused on the latest need, fad, or change in modern education. Common Core Standards, and Teaching Methods to align with the Standards, receive top billing in these days. Most keynote speakers are charismatic and entertaining, filling the room with laughter at the anecdotes supplied by moments in their teaching experiences. It is a feel-good moment, and perhaps the last of the conference before teachers are released to choose from the schedule of various "more serious" sessions located in smaller conference rooms throughout the four-star hotel.

The smaller "break-out sessions" are often delivered by "accomplished" educators who are given an hour to share "insights" they have received by applying the latest technology toward teaching Common Core Standards, using group activities for higher good, identifying obstacles toward learning in the classroom (typically it is a lack of technology), and the many glorious uses of Google for the classroom. Yes, the answer is always found in more technology, more group activities, and less teacher-led instruction. Students, we learn, are the best teachers of themselves if given a computer and a few links within a group project. *The sessions teach the teachers how to do more teaching by doing less actual teaching.*

Have I not just argued myself into a circle? Less teaching is more teaching? No, the process of educating a student is *not* a peer-peer process; the blind leading the blind inevitably leads to the cliff and a hard fall. Effective teaching is demanding and *requires* a dedicated and intelligent instructor. Such a teacher *knows* the students who make up each class; understands each student's academic ability; carefully designs and provides those students on that precise day with the best material for the specific subject matter; explains why this material rather than another has been chosen for that particular lesson; knows how and when and whom to adapt that material for throughout the lesson; and most importantly, is thoroughly familiar with and passionate about the discipline he teaches.

This cannot be accomplished by a computer nor by a mandated schedule and supplied lesson designed miles away by a Princeton University professor (likely a part-time employee or consultant for a software development educational company or testing company). Additionally, it is foolish to believe that a department, or the chair of a department, can design a schedule whereby one class lesson can be mimicked in the next class. This faulty "department"-determined lesson-planning master schedule is a dismal failure because it always places the schedule ahead of where a class might be, and every class moves at a different pace to adapt to the level of learning within that class. It is not surprising that as "experts" instruct teachers how to be a success by following their example of students teaching students or applying more computer activities, or departments working "together," students fail to reach their full potential.

Every parent knows situations arise for teaching a child, and regardless of how a parent plans to educate their child to be a well-rounded productive adult in the future, real learning takes place by recognizing the teaching moment, making use of it, reinforcing it, reteaching it if necessary, and moving on to the next opportunity as it specifically applies to their child's abilities, desires, and needs. How is it any different in the classroom, unless the classroom is thought of as an industrial factory with the end product being moved out within twelve years, flawed or not?

More professional developments, as presently designed, thus do little more than to reinforce ineffective teaching strategies, waste time and money, and unless or until they recognize the failures in the current system, their effectiveness is minimal at best and destructive at their worst.

9. What Is Effective Teaching?

I have already pointed out through multiple cases that *more* of the same is not the answer, thus begging the question, "What *should* be done?" An entire book would be required to address this question but suffice it for the sake of brevity to offer the following suggestions:Tenure must be based on more demanding requirements than time served. Teaching, as with any job, ought to reward success and also have an effective and fair process for dismissal of employees who fail to perform with measurable success. Of course, the fly in the ointment is the standard for measurement, and to expand here into details would be to digress into the material for a second book and so I will deny the impulse to expand on that topic at this point. Regarding rewards and dismissals, I suggest monetary bonuses in the form of pay, additional class-room materials, and *extended* contracts for well-performing teachers. For the underperforming teachers, a systematic plan for measurable improvement steps must be written, a master teacher ought to be assigned for assistance and evaluations on a long-term basis, and if improvement is not attained, a termination must follow.

1) Technology must offer only a supporting role. *Physical books and librar-ies* are an invaluable resource defining primary and secondary source material, guides in research, and *offer a permanency to learning which is absent in the digital age.* The immediacy of type, search, copy is the fast-food diet substituting itself for the healthier time-honored process of holding a physical book, reading, underlining, taking physical notes, using bibliographies, and in the more demanding use of time, more is retained for the effort in the process itself.

2) Human Assessments: The role of the teacher must include the role of the assessor as a primary function of the job. Note, *this does not mean the administrator of computerized exams, but rather one who personally administers questions specific to each student during instruction to gain an understanding of the student's knowledge.* Comprehensive oral examina-tions may seem antiquated and therefore unfashionable except in the Exams schools associated with ancient universities, but clearly a human instructor is more capable of testing a student's ability to reason beyond memorization, utilize critical-thinking-related higher-level questions based on previous answers, and actually use the oral exam assessment strategy to *teach* a student how to find the answer or the means to the answer. Imagine, assessing a student as a means toward learning rather than as an axe to punish the student with a fail. Far too many students have a fifteen-week semester passing grade, succeed day after day in work, and then fail the course (requiring an entire repeat) due to an over-weighted test on sixteen weeks of material. What this boils down

to is that for the sake of a *single* assessment of a *single* style given on a *single* day, a student's passing grade for sixteen or even thirty-two weeks, five days a week, a single failed exam sets a student back to day one. Not only is the student taught a false lesson about what learning or success means, that student is imprinted with a hatred for the incomprehensible subject. Perhaps it is not the subject so much as the imbalanced and prejudicial form of assessment combined with poor teaching that has revealed itself as failing.

I have often suggested that a teacher ought to be subjected to the same standard in order to learn how damaging this Final Exam single-form assessment is as a strategy. Allow a teacher to teach adequately for every day of the semester, and then on a single day at the end of the semester an administrator will assess the teacher in a manner most incongruent to that teacher's natural teaching ability, and by the failing of that single assessment, that teacher must surrender the entire semester worth of pay! How quickly would unions and teachers object and overturn such an injustice.

Is there rottenness at the heart of Common Core?

Indeed there is, and that rottenness is the idea of "more," more standardized tests, compiled by a remote and anonymous "educational soviet," to be reinforced by its commissars in continuing education and professional development workshops, while the students learn the modern digital equivalent, through copying and pasting, of finger-painting and clay-modeling.

Enough is enough.

Epilogue: Our Wings are Melting
Artificial Intelligence and the Enslavement
of the Human Mind

"The most important thing is a person. A person who incites your curiosity and feeds your curiosity; and machines cannot do that in the same way that people can."

—

Steve Jobs

---

otice that the founder of Apple did not say that machines are incapable of feeding a student's curiosity, but rather that *"machines cannot do that [feed curiosity]* **in the same way that people can.**" There is a revolution afoot and one that this book has gone to great lengths to unfold: a revolution to engineer the future generations through the institution of public education. The players, the agenda, and the means to their end have been presented. What is critical to take note of is the fact that we are now at the dawn of a potentially apocalyptic moment which was set into motion many generations ago, and for the first time we face a moment of action which is do or die, intellectually and ethically speaking; to allow the final domino in this educational revolution to fall is fatal, for it is a point from which there *is no turning back*. We repeat, there will be *no turning back*!

In the not so distant past, the social architects behind this subtle indoctrination had to battle the individual states, the local school boards, the teachers, and the parents in order to make any forward progress. The game is different with the Common Core Standards revolution, as even the architects who have uncorked the genie from the bottle are blinded by their own ambitions to the coming disaster. Again, we remind the reader that it is not the so-called Standards, but rather that the genie's nose out of the bottle is the introduction of artificial intelligence assessment, which of necessity leads to artificial intelligence machine *instruction* of human beings, and such instruction will not only be out of the hands of classroom teachers but potentially even out of the hands of the social, political, and corporate education manipulators who dreamed of their dystopian realities of elitist supremacy. The genie serves no one except itself.

The authors of this book do not stand alone in their warning of the irreversible dangers coming with the implementation of such predictive AI methods infiltrating our society and now realized in public school testing. These changes are already evident and in use for testing students in Common Core states; they are part and parcel of the Common Core agenda. Nick Bostrom, a Swedish philosopher at the University of Oxford, best known for his work on superintelligence risks (also known as AI or human-level machine intelligence) and the possibility of human extinction, presents a frightening scenario of humans competing in every aspect of life against equally intelligent machines as soon as the year 2040.[1] Take a moment to let this sink in. As machines progress toward the attainment of human-level ability to think, reason, and accomplish any task as well as any human, the student in the elementary classroom today will likely graduate into a world where the competition for a job will no longer be against the nerd or jock sitting at the table beside him, but rather against an entity whose "mind" is faster at solving problems or accomplishing tasks, whose "body" does not require health care, who does not call in sick, take maternity leave, does not retire, and who does not demand a cost-of-living increase! Any job—*every* job—can and will be done by a more efficient machine, and we are the fools announcing our rise to the top of the tower of Babel; we have not become gods by our creation of AI, we have become its future servants.

According to Bostrom, the machine with human-level intelligence will not simply reach this designed goal within the lifetime of most of our readers; rather, within "moments" of achieving this status it will move past the most brilliant mind that has ever lived and surpass human-level intelligence beyond anyone's imagination, making *it* the singular designer of humanity's future. It will be that last invention any human makes, as all future inventions,

---

1   cf. Nick Bostrom, *Superintelligence: Paths, Dangers, Strategies* (University of Oxford Press), 2014.

ideas, and the direction of humanity will be dictated by *it* due to its vastly superior ability to optimize all resources on the planet (including humans) and set the course according to its will or desire. This is **not** science fiction; it is our reality, and the implementation of its use (crude as it may be by comparison to what it will accomplish in the near future) in our schools through the Common Core Assessment process can either be a wake-up call (as is should be), or dismissal bell for parents all across the nation.

Handing over education and assessment to a "superintelligence" future is the paradigm shift from which a return to the days of humans teaching humans will be impossible. The replacement of books with computers, teachers with computer links, oral and written exams with predictive software testing programs, is ultimately the replacement of human culture with a Transhumanist (inhumane) or technocratic culture. To borrow the warning of the Greeks, Icarus has flown too high, and the inevitable fall from the heavens must follow. We are on the verge of such a fall, and yet politicians, local school boards, administrators, teachers, unions, and even many "experts" in education are announcing the great heights to which we will climb with the future generation of students using technology in the classroom! Can you feel the wings melting yet?

Where does this leave us? Bostrom cautions that the hope for humans surviving into the future is found by imputing human values and ideals into this godlike creation before the final on-switch is flipped. One wonders, which values and imputed by whom? Christian values? Muslim values? Atheistic values? What model human might be the "ideal"? Mother Theresa? Pope John Paul II? Bill Gates? The ethical dilemma of creating such a list of "values" is challenging enough, but under the best-case scenario, what if such values were infused within the operating system of our future man-made god? Would such a machine not see humans as Agent Smith saw Mr. Anderson in *The Matrix* movie trilogy, as a virus whose existence violates all the values which humans supposedly hold? In other words, for the machine to dutifully carry out the attainment of the human ideal, it might very well determine that the removal of the human race, or its enslavement, is the best means toward delivering a successful attainment of the goals humans input to the machine! From creators to servants of its creation, we stand at a moment in time where action must be taken while there is a moment to take action left to us. Our future depends upon intelligent, reasonable, and ethical action taken now.

Steve Jobs wisely understood that there is a vast difference between the curiosity inspired by a teacher and the curiosity that comes from a machine to a student. Parents understand this principle and recognize that the latest virtual-reality earth exploration program is hardly as interesting *or transforming* in the life of their child as a walk through Yosemite or an evening to stargaze atop a mountain. Parents understand that a child's discovery is intimately connected to imagination and the experiences that come from involving all of the senses in the process of learning. What is left to learn when all knowledge is a click away? What experiences are left to experience when the outcome will be predicted by a machine before the first step in learning has happened? *What possible benefit is derived when an education is an online or downloaded event void of human contact?*

There was a time when "learning" was a deliberate and reasonable (logical) human pilgrimage, when the method of teaching was relational and personal, where provocative sparks of information created pathways to new ideas, "aha" moments of discovery in students created by the intelligent calculated steps of a teacher, a teacher who knew the students nearly as well as the parent knew the child. A parent or a superior teacher who recognized the facial expressions and the body language, who knew the right moment to lead a child to ask the critical question and who would brilliantly make use of the "pause" to allow (require) that student to think, reason, and discover within themselves the litany of questions that follow before an answer is found, leading to the next round of questions to be researched. Development of character happens in the discipline of work, and an education that feeds immediate answers without the mind at work is not an education at all. It is servitude and dependence on the machine whose fast-food reply satisfies the nanosecond of curiosity with "the answer." Dare we say that "the answer" is not always "the answer," and the day has already arrived when one must be told, "Who are *you* to question Google? Do you know more than Google?" The expert is handed the silver while the machine has already taken the gold!

We must ask ourselves why would we celebrate the advent of a new era in education when that advent is an ending, not a beginning? These Common Core Standards as they are now implemented with predictive assessments and alternative online "learning" programming are the gateway to a future whose finish line is beyond any Orwellian dystopia. For fun, ask SIRI how to turn off SIRI. The answer you will receive is: "That doesn't sound very fun. How about we play the quiet game, instead."

And so, *will we* play the quiet game or will we rise to the challenge... perhaps the machine has already predicted this question and has its strategy in place; where is our strategy? Epilogue is indeed prologue.

Conant, James Bryant. *Education and Liberty: The Role of Schools in a Modern Democracy*. Cambridge, Massachusetts: Harvard University Press, 1953. No ISBN.

Conant, James Bryant. *The Revolutionary Transformation of the American High School*. Inglis Lectures in Secondary Education. Cambridge, Massachusetts: Harvard University Press, 1959. (Reprint 2013). ISBN 978-0-674-28287-2.

Counts, George S. *Dare the School Build a New Social Order?* Carbondale, Illinois: Southern Illinois University Press, 1978 (Reprint of original 1932 article). ISBN 0-8093-0878-9.

Farley, Todd. *Making the Grades: My Misadventures in the Standardized Testing Industry*. San Francisco, California: Berrett-Koehler Publishers, Inc., 2009. ISBN978-0-98170-915-4.

Garrison, Mark J. *A Measure of Failure: The Political Origins of Standardized Testing*. Albany: State University of New York Press, 2009. ISBN 978-1-4384-2776-2.

Gatto, John Taylor. *Dumbing Us Down: The Hidden Curriculum of Compulsory Schooling*. Gabriola Island, British Columbia: New Society Publishers, 2005. ISBN 978-0-86571-448-9.

Gatto, John Taylor. *Weapons of Mass Instruction: A Schoolteacher's Journey Through the Dark World of Compulsory Schooling*. Bariola Island, British Columbia: New Society Publishers, 2009. ISBN 978-0-86671-669-8.

Hoffman, Banesh. *The Tyranny of Testing*. Mineola, New York: Dover Publications, Inc., 2003. ISBN 978-0-486-43091-X.

Lemann, Nicholas. *The Big Test: The Secret History of the American Meritocracy.*
New York: Farrar, Straus and Giroux, 1999. ISBN 0-374-29984-6.

Marks, John. *The Search for the Manchurian Candidate: The CIA and Mind Control: The Secret History of the Behavioral Sciences*. New York: W.W. Norton and
Company, 1979. ISBN 978-0-393-30794-8.

Picciano, Anthony G., and Joel Spring. *The Great American Education-Industrial Complex: Ideology, Technology, and Profit*. New York: Routledge, 2013.
ISBN 978-0-415-52414-8.

Scheflin, Alan W., and Edward M. Opton, Jr. *The Mind Manipulators*. New York: Paddington Press, Ltd., 1978.

Thomson Iserbyt, Charlotte. *The Deliberate Dumbing Down of America*. Revised and Abridged Edition. Parkman, Ohio: Conscience Press, 2011.
ISBN 978-0-9667071-1-3.

Wormser, René A. *Foundations: Their Power and Influence*. New York: The Devin-Adair Company, 1958. No ISBN.

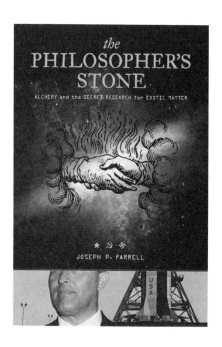

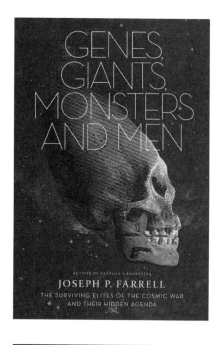

THE PHILOSOPHER'S STONE
Alchemy and Secret Research for
Exotic Matter
$17.95

The Philosopher's Stone reveals the
connections between little known
ideas in physics and ancient alchemy.
Examining American, Soviet, and Nazi
research, Farrell traces out alchemy's
view of an information-creating physical medium, and shows how this idea is
related to the phenomenon of high-spin
rotation and the unusual properties in
matter that it induces.

GENES, GIANTS, MONSTERS, & MEN
The Surviving Elites of the Cosmic War
and Their Hidden Agenda
$19.95

Consider the possibility that the history
of the human race is not as simple as
has been taught in classroom textbooks.
Consider the possibility that the standard scientific explanation for mankind
has ignored critical facts that are buried
deep within the fossils and mankind's
DNA. Consider the possibility that the
biblical tales may actually reveal an
essential truth about a planet occupied
with tyrannical giants and an elite race
bent on genetic mutation.

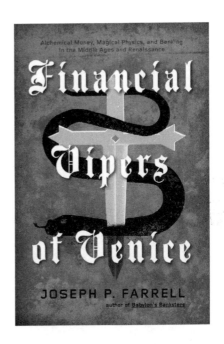

BABYLON'S BANKSTERS
*The Alchemy of Deep Physics, High
Finance and Ancient Religion*
$19.95

From ancient Babylon to Baby-
lon-on-the-Hudson, an international
class of gangster bankers—banksters—
has pursued a consistent strategy to
enslave mankind, by usurping the
money-creating and issuing power of
the state, to suppressing the public
development of alternative physics and
energy technologies.

FINANCIAL VIPERS OF VENICE
*Alchemical Money, Magical Physics,
and Banking in the Middle Ages
and Renaissance*
$19.95

In this sequel to Joseph P. Farrell's
Babylon's Banksters, the banksters have
moved from Mesopotamia via Rome to
Venice. There they have manipulated
popes and bullion prices, clipped coins,
sacked Constantinople, destroyed rival
Florence, waged war, burned "heretics,"
and suppressed hidden secrets threaten-
ing their financial supremacy.

Rotten to the (Common) Core: Public Schooling,
Standardized Tests, and the Surveillance State
© 2016 by Joseph P. Farrell and Gary Lawrence

All rights reserved
A Feral House book
ISBN 978-1-93417-0-649

Process Media
1240 W. Sims Way Suite 124
Port Townsend WA 98368
www.ProcessMediaInc.com

Book design by Jacob Covey

10 9 8 7 6 5 4 3 2 1